THE INTERNATIONAL IMPERATIVE IN HIGHE

M000032196

GLOBAL PERSPECTIVES ON HIGHER EDUCATION

Volume 27

Higher education worldwide is in a period of transition, affected by globalization, the advent of mass access, changing relationships between the university and the state, and the new technologies, among others. *Global Perspectives on Higher Education* provides cogent analysis and comparative perspectives on these and other central issues affecting postsecondary education worldwide.

Series Editor:
Philip G. Altbach
Center for International Higher Education, Boston College, USA

This series is co-published with the Center for International Higher Education at Boston College.

The International Imperative in Higher Education

By

Philip G. Altbach
Center for International Higher Education, Boston College, USA

SENSE PUBLISHERS
ROTTERDAM / BOSTON / TAIPEI

A C.I.P. record for this book is available from the Library of Congress.

ISBN 978-94-6209-336-2 (paperback)
ISBN 978-94-6209-337-9 (hardback)
ISBN 978-94-6209-338-6 (e-book)

Published by: Sense Publishers,
P.O. Box 21858, 3001 AW Rotterdam, The Netherlands
https://www.sensepublishers.com/

Printed on acid-free paper

All rights reserved © 2013 Sense Publishers

No part of this work may be reproduced, stored in a retrieval system, or transmitted in any form
or by any means, electronic, mechanical, photocopying, microfilming, recording or otherwise,
without written permission from the Publisher, with the exception of any material supplied
specifically for the purpose of being entered and executed on a computer system, for exclusive
use by the purchaser of the work.

Table of Contents

Preface

All but three of the contents in this volume appeared in *International Higher Education*, the quarterly publication of the Boston College Center for International Higher Education since 2006. Three essays appeared in *Global Briefs for Higher Education Leaders*, a collaborative project of CIHE and the American Council on Education. This book is a sequel to *International Higher Education: Reflections on Policy and Practice*, published in 2006 by CIHE and which included articles from *International Higher Education* written prior to that date.

The essays were selected for their timeliness and have not been updated for this book. In some cases, statistics and other details may have changed since original publication.

The work of the Center for International Higher Education is funded by the Lynch School of Education at Boston College, with assistance from the Carnegie Corporation of New York. We are indebted to Edith S. Hoshino, who edited all of the essays in this book as well as the Center's other publications.

Subscriptions to *International Higher Education* are available free of charge. Please access the CIHE Web site (http//www.bc.edu/cihe). *IHE* is also available in Chinese, Russian, Spanish, and Portuguese editions.

Philip G. Altbach
Chestnut Hill, Massachusetts
May 2013.

Introduction

The two main drivers of higher education transformation worldwide—massification and the global knowledge economy—continue to produce unprecedented change, making it ever more difficult to understand the nature of change and how to adjust to changing circumstance. Our aim is to illustrate key challenges in short essays highlighting key issues.

There are several "iron laws" of massification—trends that are the inevitable result of the dramatic expansion of enrollments in the past several decades. Among these are:

- Higher education, on average, has decreased in quality. As access has been widened to ever-larger groups in the population, the academic preparation and probably the native ability of many students has decreased. Less money is spent on each student, and the conditions of study have deteriorated.
- There is much greater inequality in higher education worldwide. This includes academic institutions, student access, and other aspects. Top universities, usually established institutions, remain excellent and probably on average have improved. But academic institutions at the bottom of the hierarchy have not improved and are perhaps worse. Many of these institutions are "demand absorbing" private schools with inadequate staffing and facilities.
- Massification requires a differentiated academic system with institutions serving varied needs and populations—thus there is more variability among institutions. Many countries have not yet created such systems, although they will inevitably emerge.
- On average, the quality of the academic profession has deteriorated. A growing number of academics do not have advanced degrees, and financial and other pressures have made an academic career unattractive to the "best and brightest."
- The private sector, much of it for-profit, expands dramatically, now accounting for a majority of enrollments in many countries. With notable exceptions, the quality of the new private sector is poor.

Globalization also produces realities that affect higher education.

- An international knowledge network—dependent on the Internet, increased use of English as the main scientific language, and growing linkages among academic institutions—is a central reality of academe.
- Universities, especially those at the top of the academic system, are increasingly part of the global knowledge network.
- The traditional academic centers, especially in the large English-speaking countries, dominate the world system; and many

universities especially in the developing world find themselves involved but peripheral in the network.

- International student mobility increases, with flows largely from developing and middle-income countries to the traditional academic centers.
- The "brain drain"—what is commonly referred to as brain exchange—also expands, flowing largely from developing and middle-income countries to the main centers, in North America and Europe for the most part, although there is considerable variation—such as within the Middle East.

The articles included here reflect a set of academic values, and thus many have a "point of view." I see higher education as a "public good"—benefiting the entire society as well as individuals. Thus, higher education deserves support and funding by society because universities benefit society as well as the individual. Increasingly, "private good" arguments dominate debate about higher education, with the result that individuals are increasingly asked to pay most of the cost of higher education, the private higher education sector has expanded dramatically, and public universities are privatized as public funding is reduced. In part this trend is an inevitable result of massification as governments are unable to pay the full cost of mass higher education systems; but the private good philosophy strengthens the trend toward privatization, much to the detriment of traditional academic values.

Linked to a commitment to the public good, there is a certain skepticism concerning a growing commercialism in higher education, as well as a belief that a "not for profit" orientation serves academic institutions, students, the professoriate, and society. The rise of the "for profit" higher education sector, the increasing commercialism of international education programs, and similar trends do not seem to be in the long-term-based interests of higher education.

The dramatic increase in inequality in global higher education is seen as a problem and a negative trend. In particular, the disadvantages faced by academic institutions and systems in the developing world, are deeply problematic. These inequalities result from basic structural factors for the most part but are exacerbated in some ways by globalization.

The essays in this book focus on a range of issues that have global relevance. Some discuss how individual countries cope with certain central global challenges, while others analyze key global realities—academic mobility and the brain drain, the challenges faced by the professoriate, aspects of globalization such as the impact of agents and recruiters in student mobility, and branch campuses and franchising—academic freedom and a special concern with the two largest academic systems (India and China).

1

The Imperial Tongue: English as the Dominating Academic Language

The English language dominates science, scholarship, and instruction as never before. While it is unlikely that English will achieve the status that Latin had as the sole language of teaching and scholarship at the 13th-century universities in Europe, the Latin analogy has some relevance today. Back then, Latin not only permitted the internationalization of universities but allowed the Roman Catholic Church to dominate intellectual and academic life. It was only the Protestant Reformation led by Martin Luther, combined with a growing sense of national identity, that challenged and then displaced Latin with national languages. As late as the 1930s, German was a widely used international scientific language. Until the mid-20th century, most countries used their national languages for university teaching and for science and scholarship. French, German, Russian, and Spanish were, and to some extent still are, used for academic and scientific publications and have some regional sway. Scholarly communities in Japanese, Chinese, Swedish, and many other languages continue to exist as well. English was the closest thing to an international language, with several major academic systems using it—the United States, Britain, Australia, New Zealand, and most of Canada. In addition, the emerging academic systems of the former British Empire—especially India, Pakistan, South Africa, and Nigeria—have traditionally used English as the main teaching and publishing language. But English did not dominate scholarly communication until the 1950s, and national academic communities seemed in general committed to national languages.

English now serves unchallenged as the main international academic language. Indeed, national academic systems enthusiastically welcome English as a contributor to internationalizing, competing, and becoming "world class." But the domination by English moves world science toward hegemony led by the main English-speaking academic systems and creates difficulties for scholars and universities that do not use English.

Origins of English Hegemony

It is not hard to see why English is the dominant academic and scientific language. The nations using English, particularly the United States, have become the academic superpowers. Size and wealth matter a great deal in determining the academic pecking order. The United States alone spends almost half the world's R&D funds and is home to a large proportion of the top universities on the world's increasingly influential league tables. The English-speaking academic systems host more than half the world's international students. Many of these graduates return to their home countries with a zeal for English and for the foreign universities at which they obtained their degrees. The main scientific and scholarly journals are published in English because their editors and most of their contributors are professors at universities in the English-speaking countries. Similarly, the large majority of the world's academic Web sites and scientific networks function in English.

English is the world's most widely studied second language. This gives English a significant advantage in many non-English-speaking countries simply because of the number of speakers and the fact that English is by far the most widely distributed language. There are, for example, more students studying English in China than are studying English in the United States and more speakers of English in India than in Britain. Further, English has an official governmentally recognized status in more than 70 countries. Colonialism provided stimulus for the spread of English (as well as other European languages) as early as the 18th century—to North America, South Asia, and the Caribbean—and later to Africa, other parts of Asia, Australasia, and the South Pacific. Today, no African university offers instruction in any indigenous African language, and academic and intellectual life takes place in English, French, Portuguese, Arabic, and Afrikaans.

Evidence of English Hegemony

The international role of English and its growing role in academic life worldwide have many implications. The power of English-language scientific and scholarly journals means that the research paradigms and scholarly interests of the journal editors, editorial board members, and indeed the majority of readers control journals and to a large extent research agendas and methodologies in most disciplines. Scholars in other parts of the world must conform to the interests of the prestigious journals if they wish their work to be published in them. While the Internet is more open, the interests of the major contributors and users tend to dominate, and the English language is most widely used. International scientific meetings increasingly use English as the only official language.

The curriculum is increasingly dominated by the major English-speaking countries, and in a globalized world this means that curricular developments are expressed in English and increasingly come from the United States and a few other countries. The international proliferation of the master of business administration degree (MBA) is a good example of how academic programs spread. The MBA degree was developed in the United States to serve the needs of American business and became the standard qualification required by senior executives. In the past two decades, English has become recognized as a key qualification for management in other countries, compelled both by the growing influence of multinational corporations and by the power of American universities. US universities now offer MBA degrees in many parts of the world, and non-US universities have established their own MBA programs, often using English and a largely US curriculum. This development shows the power both of the English language and of American higher education practices and ideas.

The academic journals and books published in English and edited from the United States and the United Kingdom increasingly dominate world scholarship. These publications are almost the only ones internationally circulated. They are the most prestigious journals, and academics worldwide compete to publish in them. They are listed in the Science Citation Index and its sister indexes. While SCI was not developed to rank journals or to measure the scholarly productivity of individual academics or institutions but rather to trace how scientific ideas become influential and are communicated, it has become a de facto ranking. Universities worldwide want their professors to publish in these listed journals and reward those who do. For example, Norwegian academics who publish in English and in recognized journals are paid fees for their accomplishments, while their colleagues who publish in Norwegian are paid less or not at all. In Korea, great pressures are placed on academics to publish in recognized international journals in English. Publication in English and in internationally recognized journals and by prestigious international publishers counts more than publishing elsewhere.

Academic programs offered in English have become widespread in many non-English-speaking countries. Universities in Europe, Asia, and Latin America are offering degree programs in English alongside instruction in national languages. A small number of new private universities operating solely in English have also been established, sometimes calling themselves the American University of . . . to take advantage of the prestige and popularity of English. In some cases, these universities seek accreditation in the United States, and for a few such institutions accreditation has been granted.

The worldwide branch campus movement for the most part uses English as the medium of instruction. The United States, Australia, and the United Kingdom have been most active in establishing branch campuses, and it is not surprising that English is the medium of instruction. Non-English-speaking countries often use English as well. Dutch and German branch overseas campuses often offer their programs in English. There are at least 100 branch campuses, mainly sponsored by universities in the North and operating in the South. The branch campus movement exports both language and curriculum, introducing new ideas into host countries and perhaps displacing national models.

Most observers see the impact of English in higher education worldwide as a positive trend—contributing to globalization and enhancing an international academic culture. A global academic environment needs a common medium of communication, and English is the only possible language. While English brings new ideas to sometimes moribund academic institutions worldwide, there are significant downsides to the new hegemony of English.

Downsides

The impact of English increases the influence of the major English-speaking academic systems, particularly of the United States and the United Kingdom. These countries have many of the world's leading universities, produce a high proportion of scientific discoveries and scholarship, and form the centers of scientific communication. The norms, values, methodologies, and orientations of the academic communities of these centers tend to dominate the rest of the world—the peripheries.

What happens to national scientific communities in an English-dominated global environment? There has always been a tension between the local and the global in science and scholarship—since knowledge is by its nature international. The use of national languages and the existence of national journals and publishers are called into question by policymakers and academic administrators worldwide. Knowledge is ranked according to whether it is recognized by the international academic community or not. If not, even though a domestic publication may be highly relevant to national needs, it is considered even within a country as being less prestigious, and this may have implications for a scholar's academic career or salary. Ambitious academics will naturally seek to publish in international publications to advance their impact and careers. Topics such as local history or research on local health problems may be ignored to gain recognition internationally.

Some time ago, the Dutch minister of education proposed that universities in the Netherlands shift the language of instruction from Dutch to English so that Holland could boost its attraction for international students and integrate more fully into the global scholarly community. The Dutch Parliament debated the issue and decided not to shift the language—arguing that the Netherlands would lose its distinctive culture if the Dutch language was no longer used for intellectual and academic life. This argument is relevant elsewhere. If the knowledge that is most valued is aimed at the international academic world and is communicated in English, there will be negative implications for national scientific and intellectual systems.

In many countries, academic rewards of all kinds accrue to those using English and participating in global scientific networks. These scholars are typically invited to international conferences, awarded research funds by both international and national funders, and are generally seen as leaders of their scientific communities. Universities and governments often use the SCI and related systems to judge the impact and value of their academics and universities. SCI becomes a kind of proxy for quality and productivity. Similarly, the international ranking systems use such measures. However, again, this offers privileges those who produce their work in English and intend to reach an international audience.

These factors will tend to orient researchers and scholars to themes that they feel will appeal to an international audience, often at the expense of essential but more parochial themes that might be of interest only to local or national audiences. Further, the methodologies chosen for research will follow those popular internationally, whether these methods are relevant to the specific topic being researched.

The current debate concerning the General Agreement on Trade in Services (GATS) as part of the World Trade Organization (WTO) has direct implications for this discussion. GATS will force academic systems worldwide to be more open to foreign influences. Should GATS be widely implemented, this will inevitably mean the English-language institutions and programs will further entrench themselves worldwide.

These factors lead to homogenizing knowledge worldwide. Not only is English the dominant language, but its relationship with the controlling trends in international science and scholarship is a powerful combination of forces contributing to decreasing diversity of themes and methodologies.

What Can Be Done?

If globalization determines the direction of the world economy, science, and other factors, then the growth of English as the global language of science and scholarship is inevitable for the foreseeable future. Science indeed is increasingly international, and the global mobility of students and professors is a long-term reality. There is an international knowledge network that involves not only science and scholarship but increasingly people. This network operates mainly in English and is dominated by the main English-speaking academic systems.

The argument here is that the international network is both inevitable and largely positive but that national and local scientific communities and higher education systems must be protected. These communities deserve both respect and support because they bring a valuable perspective and diversity to science and scholarship. Internationalization may be positive but with homogenization we lose a concern for local and regional issues as well as ideas that may not be in the international mainstream. An entirely open market will weaken these communities, just as the major world languages today are snuffing out small and weak languages. Science and scholarship in national languages deserve support. The evaluation of academic merit should not depend solely on the rankings of the SCI or other exogenous agencies—and thus left to judgment of foreigners. While local evaluation may not be easy, it is necessary. An appropriate mix between local and international publication will help nurture an active research community.

The essential necessity is an understanding of the importance of national scientific and intellectual communities. Creating a balance between the local and the global may not be easy but intellectual independence depends on it.

[*IHE* 49, Fall 2007]

2

Globalization and Forces for Change in Higher Education

What is globalization and how does it affect higher education policy and academic institutions? The answer is deceivingly simple and the implications are surprisingly complex. For higher education, globalization implies the broad social, economic, and technological forces that shape the realities of the 21st century. These elements include advanced information technology, new ways of thinking about financing higher education and a concomitant acceptance of market forces and commercialization, unprecedented mobility for students and professors, the global spread of common ideas about science and scholarship, the role of English as the main international language of science, and other developments. Significantly, the idea of mass access to higher education has meant unprecedented expansion of higher education everywhere—there are about 134 million students in postsecondary education worldwide, and many countries have seen unprecedented and sustained expansion in the past several decades. These global trends are for the most part inevitable. Nations, and academic institutions, must constructively cope with the implications.

Contemporary inequalities may in fact be intensified by globalization. Academic systems and institutions that at one time could grow within national boundaries now find themselves competing internationally. National languages compete with English even within national borders. Domestic academic journals, for example, often compete with international publications within national academic systems, and scholars are pressured to publish internationally. Developing countries are at a significant disadvantage in the new globalized academic system, but smaller academic systems in rich countries also face problems. In a ranking-obsessed world, the top universities are located predominantly in the United States, the United Kingdom, and a few other rich countries. The inequalities of the global age are just as profound and in part more complex than the realities of the era of colonialism.

Academic systems will need to cope with the key realities of the first part of the 21st century for higher education.

Massification

Massification is without question the most ubiquitous global influence of the past half century or more. The United States had the first mass higher education system, beginning as early as the 1920s. Europe followed in the 1960s, and parts of Asia a decade or so later. The developing countries were the last to expand. Most of the growth of the 21st century is taking place in developing and middle-income countries. There are now more than 140 million students in postsecondary education worldwide, and this number continues to expand rapidly. North America, Europe, and a number of Pacific Rim nations now enroll 60 percent or more of the relevant age group in higher education. What has massification brought?

Public good vs. private good. Stimulated in part by the financial pressures of massification and also by broader changes in economic thinking, including the neoliberal agenda, higher education is increasingly considered in economic terms a private good—a benefit accruing mainly to individuals who should pay for it rather than a public good that contributes benefits to society and thus should be financially supported by the state.

Access. Postsecondary education has opened its doors to previously excluded population groups—women; people from lower socioeconomic classes; previously disadvantaged racial, religious, and ethnic groups; and other populations. While many countries still contain disparities in enrollment, massification has clearly meant access and thus upward mobility and increased earning potential. Access also greatly expanded the skills of populations, making economic expansion possible.

Differentiation. All mass higher education systems are differentiated systems. Institutions serve varied missions, with differing funding sources and patterns and a range of quality. Successful academic systems must ensure that the various segments of the system are supported and sustained. While research universities need special attention, mass-access institutions do as well.

Varied funding patterns. For most countries, the state has traditionally been the main funder of higher education. Massification has placed great strains on state funding, and in all cases governments no longer believe they can adequately fund mass higher education. Other sources of funding need to be found—including student tuition and fees (typically the largest source), a variety of government-sponsored and private loan programs, university income generating programs (such as industry collaboration or consulting), and philanthropic support.

Decline in quality and conditions of study. On average in most countries, the quality of higher education has declined. In a mass system, top quality cannot be provided to all students. It is not affordable, and the ability levels of both students and professors necessarily become more diverse. University study and teaching are no longer a preserve for the elite—both in terms of ability and wealth. While the top of a diversified academic system may maintain its quality (although in some countries the top sector has also suffered), the system, as a whole, declines.

Peaks and Valleys In Global Science and Scholarship

A variety of forces have combined to make science and scholarship global. Two key elements are responsible. The growth of information technology (IT) has created a virtual global community of scholarship and science. The increasing dominance of English as the key language of communicating academic knowledge is enhanced by IT. Global science provides everyone immediate access to the latest knowledge. Thus, everyone must compete on the same playing field to participate in research and discovery. It is as if some teams (the wealthiest universities) have the best training and equipment, while the majority of players (universities in developing countries and smaller institutions everywhere) are far behind. There is increased pressure to participate in the international big leagues of science—such as publishing in recognized journals in English. Thus, while IT makes communication easier it tends to concentrate power in the hands of the "haves" to the disadvantage of the "have nots." National or even regional academic communities, located in the valleys of higher education, are overshadowed by the peaks of the global academic powers that dominate the new knowledge networks.

Globalization of the Academic Marketplace

More than 2 million students are studying abroad, and it is estimated that this number will increase to 8 million by 2025. Many others are enrolled in branch campuses and twinning programs. There are many thousands of visiting scholars and postdocs studying internationally.

Most significantly, there is a global circulation of academics. Ease of transportation, IT, the use of English, and the globalization of the curriculum have tremendously increased the international circulation of academic talent. Flows of students and scholars move largely from South to North—from the developing countries to North America and Europe. And while the "brain drain" of the past has become more of a "brain exchange," with flows of both people and knowledge back and forth across borders and among societies, the great advantage still accrues to the traditional academic centers at the expense of the peripheries. Even China, and to some extent India, with both large and increasingly sophisticated academic systems, find themselves at a significant disadvantage in the global academic marketplace. For much of Africa, the traditional brain drain remains largely a reality.

Conclusion

Thomas Friedman's "flat world" is a reality for the rich countries and universities. The rest of the world still finds itself in a traditional world of centers and peripheries, of peaks and valleys and involved in an increasingly difficult struggle to catch up and compete with those who have the greatest academic power. In some ways, globalization works against the desire to create a worldwide academic community based on cooperation and a shared vision of academic development. The globalization of science and scholarship, ease of communication, and the circulation of the best academic talent worldwide have not led to equality in higher education. Indeed, both within national academic systems and globally, inequalities are greater than ever.

[*IHE* 50, Winter 2008]

3

The Complexities of Global Engagement

Once upon a time, not long ago, till the end of the 20th century, most American colleges and universities either did not think about global engagement and internationalization or considered study abroad as the beginning and end of such involvement. Just two decades later, global engagement stands at the top of the agenda of many academic institutions, and the scope of internationalization on campuses has expanded dramatically. It is time to consider the scope and nature of global engagement.

Uwe Brandenburg and Hans de Wit (*International Higher Education*, Winter 2011) argued that globalization, with its assumptions of economic inequality and competition, has become the evil twin of internationalization, which they see as a positive force. They point out that most aspects of global engagement and internationalization have taken on competitive and often commercial elements, and that a careful reconsideration of strategies and purposes is required. A recent meeting of G8 (group of 8 major economies) higher education officials exhibited an interesting contrast between the national strategies of the Anglo-Saxon countries and those of continental Europe. The English-speaking countries increasingly see international higher education involvement as a commercial venture, while a German official claimed—"The goal we have is to win friends for Germany," through international education strategies.

In the era of complex 21st-century global engagement, many institutions are neglecting the traditional aspects of internationalization—providing a positive overseas experience for undergraduates, encouraging international faculty research, and ensuring that foreign students, postdocs, and visiting scholars have a positive experience and contribute to campus life. While it may seem old-fashioned to think about these elements, they are as important as ever—and remain at the core of global engagement. While there is emphasis on increasing the numbers of domestic students going abroad, in some cases less attention is paid to the quality of that overseas experience. Similarly, visiting scholars are welcomed but often forgotten once they are on campus. To fulfill its promise and potential, global engagement must be a two-way street.

A Campus Foreign Policy

Global engagement encompasses a vast range of activities, which seldom add up to a coherent strategy on campus. While many universities have included internationalization as part of institutional strategy, few schools go beyond platitudes. Few define the nature of global engagement or internationalization, and few operationalize how broad goals might be achieved. Seldom is a budget or staffing linked to whatever goals may be expressed.

Academic institutions need a foreign policy. Such a policy needs to answer fundamental questions about motivations and means, aspirations and expectations. Most important, *why* is the university involved? What kinds of initiatives should be undertaken? What parts of the world should receive priority? Is the focus on research or teaching? Is the focus on faculty, graduate students, or undergraduates, and in what proportions? How are initiatives to be funded?

A foreign policy will identify specific parts of the world with which to engage, as no university can cover the entire globe. Choices may be guided by past involvement with particular countries, strong academic programs with specific international connections or aspirations, or external support (e.g., donors' priorities).

A foreign policy must be realistic. Is there campus expertise on a particular part of the world? Are there appropriate financial resources available? Is there sufficient support from targeted overseas partners? Are there appropriate personnel on campus to ensure the success of relevant initiatives?

A foreign policy is a strategic vision, not a detailed blueprint of specific activities and programs. It is intended to guide the parameters of engagement. For example, if the strategy emphasizes Asia, but a professor, or even a donor, wants to focus institutional attention on Africa, there will be a rationale for responding to proposals and making decisions. Likewise, if the foreign policy emphasizes institutional collaboration overseas, a free-standing, branch-campus initiative is unlikely to be desirable but at least can be evaluated with clear priorities in mind. The point is that a foreign policy will drive broad institutional policy.

The Advent of Commercialism

Despite a "free market" reputation in some quarters, few American colleges or universities have traditionally seen international activities in primarily commercial terms. A few large universities have long conducted money-earning international operations, and some small schools have relied on foreign students to fulfill enrollment targets. But most institutions have viewed global engagement in educational terms—when they have thought about it at all.

This is changing. At least one large American university system has emphasized the financial advantages of international activities, and many institutions are ramping up overseas enrollments, particularly from China. Links with for-profit providers of all kinds—to do recruiting overseas and to run "pathways" programs on campus for underprepared foreign undergraduates, among others—are increasingly common.

The commercialism on campus of international initiatives will inevitably create tensions between academic values and financial considerations. Will the institution cut corners to admit unqualified international students to fulfill enrollment targets? Will international students be provided with needed, and sometimes costly, support services? Will qualified domestic students be squeezed out to make room for high-fee paying international students? Will an international partnership be based principally on income-earning potential rather than on sound academic principles? All of these issues have, in fact, already been reported.

None of this is surprising in the age of state budget cuts and academic capitalism; but commercially focused global engagement is fraught with challenges—to the "brand name" among others—and may not succeed. The global image of American higher education may well change in the eyes of the international higher education community, as has happened to some extent to Australia.

Global Engagement and the Academic Community

All too often, campus international initiatives come from the top or from the interest of one or a small group of faculty. Effective global engagement requires a "buy in" and commitment from all relevant institutional stakeholders. Relevant constituencies must be fully engaged. The faculty is the key group, since they must inevitably implement any international strategy. Faculty approval is also necessary; strong opposition among vocal sections of the academic community can jeopardize initiatives. Without faculty commitment, most kinds of global engagement will either fail or will create unwanted controversy on campus.

A Commitment to the Long Haul
Often ignored in discussions of global engagement is the necessity of ensuring sustainability. Is there appropriate support on campus in terms of staff with relevant expertise? Is funding available—not just to launch a program, but to keep it going over time? Is faculty and student interest lasting? And does the foreign policy provide the effective framework for a global engagement effort that will stand the test of time?

Global engagement must be a central element of successful colleges and universities worldwide. The issues and strategies are, however, complex. Success requires a careful assessment of goals and depends on the specific realities of the institution and the academic community. A foreign policy brings together all parts of the campus community, in a coherent and realistic program. Good strategies, as with many other valuable products, do not grow on trees.

[*International Briefs for Higher Education Leaders 2*, 2012]

4

Corruption: A Key Challenge to Internationalization

A specter of corruption is haunting the global campaign toward higher education internationalization. An overseas degree is increasingly valuable, so it is not surprising that commercial ventures have found opportunities on the internationalization landscape. New private actors have entered the sector, with the sole goal of making money. Some of them are less than honorable. Some universities look at internationalization as a contribution to the financial "bottom line," in an era of financial cutbacks. The rapidly expanding private higher education sector globally is largely for-profit. In a few cases, such as Australia and increasingly the United Kingdom, national policies concerning higher education internationalization tilt toward earning income for the system.

Countries whose academic systems suffer from elements of corruption are increasingly involved in international higher education—sending large numbers of students abroad, establishing relationships with overseas universities, and other activities. Corruption is not limited to countries that may have a reputation for less than fully circumspect academic practices, but that problem occurs globally. Several scandals have recently been widely reported in the United States, including the private unaccredited "Tri-Valley University," a sham institution that admitted and collected tuition from foreign students. That institution did not require them to attend class, but rather funneled them into the labor market, under the noses of US immigration authorities. In addition, several public universities have been caught admitting students, with substandard academic qualifications. Quality-assurance agencies in the United Kingdom have uncovered problems with "franchised" British-degree programs, and similar scandals have occurred in Australia. A prominent example is the University of Wales, which was the second-largest university in the United Kingdom, with 70,000 students enrolled in 130 colleges around the world. It had to close its highly profitable degree validation program, which accounted for nearly two-thirds of institutional revenue.

With international higher education now a multibillion dollar industry around the world, individuals, countries, and institutions depending on income, prestige, and access—it is not surprising that corruption is a growing problem. If something is not done to ensure probity in international relationships in higher education, an entire structure—built on trust, a commitment to mutual understanding, and benefits for students and researchers—a commitment built informally over decades will collapse. There are signs that it is already in deep trouble.

Examples and Implications

A serious and unsolved problem is the prevalence of unscrupulous agents and recruiters funneling unqualified students to universities worldwide. A recent example was featured in Britain's *Daily Telegraph* (June 26, 2012) of an agent in China caught on video, offering to write admissions essays and to present other questionable help in admission to prominent British universities. No one knows the extent of the problem, although consistent news reports indicate that it is widespread, particularly in countries that send large numbers of students abroad, including China and India. Without question, agents now receive millions of dollars in commissions paid by the universities and, in some egregious cases, money from the clients as well. In Nottingham University's case the percentage of students recruited through agents has increased from 19 percent of the intake in 2005 to 25 percent in 2011, with more than £1 million going to the agents.

Altered and fake documents have long been a problem in international admissions. Computer design and technology exacerbate it. Fraudulent documents have become a minor industry in some parts of the world, and many universities are reluctant to accept documents from institutions that have been tainted with incidents of counterfeit records. For example, a number of American universities no longer accept applications from some Russian students—because of widespread perceptions of fraud, document tampering, and other problems. Document fraud gained momentum due to commission-based agents who have an incentive to ensure that students are "packaged" with impressive credentials, as their commissions depend on successful student placement. Those responsible for checking the accuracy of transcripts, recommendations, and degree certificates face an increasingly difficult task. Students who submit valid documentation are placed as a disadvantage since they are subjected to extra scrutiny.

Examples of tampering with and falsifying results of the Graduate Record Examination and other commonly required international examinations used for admissions have resulted in the nullifying of scores, and even cancelling examinations in some countries and regions, as well as rethinking whether on-line testing is practical. This situation has made it more difficult for students to apply to foreign universities and has made the task of evaluating students for admission more difficult.

Several countries, including Russia and India, have announced that they will be using the *Times Higher Education* and Academic Ranking of World Universities (Shanghai rankings), as a way of determining the legitimacy of foreign universities for recognizing foreign degrees, determining eligibility for academic collaborations, and other aspects of international higher education relations. This is unfortunate, since many excellent academic institutions are not included in these rankings, which mostly measure research productivity. No doubt, Russia and India are concerned about the quality of foreign partners and find the rankings convenient.

Several "host" countries have tightened up rules and oversight of cross-border student flows in response to irregularities and corruption. The US Department of State announced in June 2012 that visa applicants from India would be subjected to additional scrutiny as a response to the "Tri-Valley scandal." Earlier, both Australia and Britain changed rules and policy. Corruption is making internationalization more difficult for the entire higher education sector. It is perhaps significant that continental Europe seems to have been less affected by shady practices—perhaps in part because international higher education is less commercialized and profit driven.

The Internet has become the "Wild West" of academic misrepresentation and chicanery. It is easy to set up an impressive Web site and exaggerate the quality or lie about an institution. Some institutions claim accreditation that does not exist. There are even "accreditation mills" to accredit universities that pay a fee. A few include pictures of impressive campuses that are simply photo-shopped from other universities.

What Can Be Done?

With international higher education now big business and with commercial gain an ever-increasing motivation for international initiatives, the problems mentioned are likely to persist. However, a range of initiatives can ameliorate the situation. The higher education community can recommit to the traditional "public good" values of internationalization, although current funding challenges may make this difficult in some countries. The International Association of Universities' recent report, "Affirming Academic Values in Internationalization of Higher Education," is a good start. The essential values of the European Union's Bologna Initiatives are also consistent with the best values of internationalization. Nottingham University, mentioned earlier, provides transparency, concerning its use of agents. It supervises those it hires and, in general, adheres to best practice—as do some other universities in the United Kingdom and elsewhere.

Accreditation and quality assurance are essential for ensuring that basic quality is recognized. Agencies and the international higher education community must ensure that universities were carefully evaluated and that the results of assessment are easily available to the public and the international stakeholders.

Governmental, regional, and international agencies must coordinate their efforts and become involved in maintaining standards and protecting the image of the higher education sector. Contradictions abound. For example, the United States Department of State's Education USA seeks to protect the sector, while the Department of Commerce sees higher education just as an export commodity. Government agencies in the United Kingdom and Australia seem also to be mainly pursuing commercial interests.

Consciousness-raising about ethics and good practice in international higher education and awareness of emerging problems and continuing challenges deserve continuing attention. Prospective students and their families, institutional partners considering exchanges and research, and other stakeholders must be more sophisticated and vigilant concerning decision making. The Boston College Center for International Higher Education's Corruption Monitor is the only clearinghouse for information, relating directly to corrupt practices; additional sources of information and analysis will be helpful.

The first step in solving a major challenge to higher education internationalization is recognition of the problem itself. The higher education community itself is by no means united; and growing commercialization makes some people reluctant to act in ways that may threaten profits. There are individuals within the academic community who lobby aggressively to legitimize dubious practices. Yet, if nothing is done, the higher education sector worldwide will suffer and the impressive strides taken toward internationalization will be threatened.

[*Author's note:* I acknowledge comments from Rahul Choudaha and Liz Reisberg. *IHE* 69, Fall 2012]

5

Access Means Inequality

It seems a contradiction that access would bring inequality to higher education, but that trend is the usual case. Students, and institutions, while catering to mass access, provide vastly different quality, facilities, and focus than do elite institutions at the top, and this gulf has widened as access has expanded worldwide. Furthermore, mass higher education has, for a majority of students worldwide, lowered quality and increased dropout rates. All of these consequences have become inevitable and logical. These effects do not argue against access but rather call for a more realistic understanding of the implications of massification and the steps needed to ameliorate the problems created by dramatic increases in enrollments.

Mass higher education now forms a worldwide phenomenon. Enrollments constitute more than 150 million worldwide, having increased by 53 percent in just a decade. Twenty-six percent of the age group now participates in postsecondary education globally, up from 19 percent in 2000. In many of the rich countries, access is over half and in some over 80 percent, and in much of the developing world enrollments are dramatically increasing. This increase in access has been universally hailed—contributing to social mobility for individuals, the expansion of the knowledge economy of nations, and an increase in skill levels worldwide. In the first decade of the 21st century, quite likely more students will study in academic institutions than in the previous 10 centuries combined.

Massification has moved largely from the developed countries, which have achieved high participation rates, to developing and some middle-income nations. In fact, the majority of enrollment growth in the coming several decades will take place in two countries—China and India. China enrolls about 23 percent and India around 12 percent of the age cohort. The region with the lowest enrollment rate, sub-Saharan Africa, which in 2007 was educating only 6 percent of the age group, is expanding access but has a long way to go.

The Consequences of Access

Access brings a series of inevitable changes to higher education systems. The specific impacts and conditions will vary by location, but all countries experience these factors to some extent. Countries that have more financial resources, a strong commitment to postsecondary education, and perhaps a slower growth curve may be less dramatically affected than others; but the impact is universal and of great relevance to policymakers and the higher education community.

Student populations not only expand but also become more diverse. Traditionally, universities educated only a small elite—often fewer than 5 percent of the age group. These students came from top-secondary schools and from well-educated and affluent families. Access opens higher education to young people from an array of social class and educational backgrounds, to students from rural backgrounds, and to students who are the first in their families to study at higher education institutions. One of the most dramatic implications of greater access constitutes the expansion of women's enrollments. Women are now the majority of students in many countries. Serving students from diverse backgrounds and generally without a high-quality secondary education is a challenge. Serving these students is often more expensive than educating a small elite because tutoring, counseling, and other services are needed but are seldom available. At one time, universities assumed that almost all of the small student populations they were educating had obtained a high-quality secondary education and were prepared for academic study. Expanded access has delivered many students who have neither the academic background nor the ability that was once the norm.

Expanded access obviously requires more facilities. Existing universities and other postsecondary institutions have expanded, new institutions have been built, but supply can seldom keep up with demand. Deterioration in the conditions of study for students is common if not universal. Overcrowding, inadequate libraries and other study facilities, and the inability to provide students with the courses needed to graduate constitute familiar circumstances.

The academic profession has been stretched to the breaking point. Close to half of those teaching in postsecondary education worldwide possess only a bachelor's degree. Class sizes have increased, and students receive little personal attention from professors. Academic salaries have deteriorated, and many academics must hold more than one job to survive. It is likely that access has produced, on average, a poorer learning environment for students, in part because the academic profession has not grown fast enough to keep up with expansion.

Demand for access has contributed to the rise of private higher education in many countries. Governments have been unable to fund public-postsecondary institutions to meet expanding enrollments, and the private sector has taken up the slack. In much of Latin America, where public universities dominated the sector two decades ago, private institutions now educate half or more of the students. Most of the new private institutions are "demand absorbing"—unselective and often poor-quality schools providing a degree and little else. Many are for-profit. First-generation students may be forced to attend these new private schools, which often charge relatively high tuition, because they cannot gain access to the public sector.

Massification has created the demand for quality assurance and accreditation, but few countries have been able to set up and enforce effective regimes to ensure appropriate quality standards. This environment means that at least for the present there is little transparency or knowledge about the effectiveness of much of higher education provision, particularly at institutions that serve a mass clientele.

Access growth has meant a significant increase in noncompletion rates in higher education. Even in the United States, the country that developed the first mass higher education system and allocated significant resources to higher education, the proportion has increased significantly of students who take more than the standard four years to complete an undergraduate degree or who do not complete any degree. Many countries are unable to cope with increased demand and routinely "flunk out" a significant proportion of entering students.

Access has increased the cost of higher education—to society, individuals, and families. In much of the world, the increased cost has fallen on those who can least afford it—first-generation students and those from lower-income families. Governments cannot afford to fund access and have increased the cost of study or turned over expansion to the private sector.

The Inevitability of Inequality
The reality of postsecondary education, in an era of access combined with fiscal constraint and ever-increasing costs, is that inequality within higher education systems is here to stay. Most countries have or are

creating differentiated systems of higher education that will include different kinds of institutions serving specific needs. This process is inevitable and largely positive. However, the research universities at the top of any system tend to serve an elite clientele and have high status, while institutions lower in the hierarchy cater to students who cannot compete for the limited seats at the top. Major and growing differences exist in funding, quality, and facilities within systems. Given financial and staffing constraints, institutional inequalities will continue. Students will come from more diverse backgrounds and in many ways will be more difficult to serve effectively.

All of these issues constitute a deep contradiction for 21st-century higher education. As access expands, inequalities within the higher education system also grow. Conditions of study for many students deteriorate. More of them fail to obtain degrees. The economic benefits assumed to accrue to persons with a postsecondary qualification probably decline for many. Access remains an important goal—and an inevitable goal—of higher education everywhere, but it creates many challenges.

[IHE 61, Fall 2012]

6

What International Advice Do Universities Need?*

The latest accouterment of world-class universities, or those aspiring to world-class status, is an international advisory group. Heidelberg University, in Germany, has one headed by a former Oxford vice chancellor; the Higher School of Economics committee, in Moscow, is chaired by a Nobel Prize–winning American economist; and several prominent Saudi Arabian universities have committees composed of top-ranking academics and a few business executives. The launch of national Excellence Initiatives in various parts of the world—China, France, Germany, the Russian Federation, Spain, and South Korea, to mention only a few—has often been associated with the creation of such advisory boards at the institutional level.

The laudable goals of such committees, which meet on an occasional basis to review and evaluate the institution's plans and performance, include bringing new ideas and analysis from the experience of academe beyond the borders and especially from the pinnacles of higher education globally, and hopefully assist the institution to understand itself and to improve. The committee members have a continuing relationship with the university and, presumably, a commitment to its welfare and improvement. They can be called on for occasional advice, generally on a pro bono basis.

These committees may also bring added prestige to the university. A distinguished group of internationally respected academics provides

---

* With Jamil Salmi

luster—having connections with a Nobel Prize winner helps, even if in an advisory group.

Such committees meet once or twice a year, usually at the university, and their sessions are typically attended by the top management of the university. Sessions last for a day or two and often include a consideration—not only of the broad performance and plans of the institution but often a specific analysis of one or more programs, departments, or initiatives thought to be worth detailed consideration.

Who Serves—and Why?

Although not based on a careful and systematic analysis of advisory-committee membership, it appears that most committees consist of prominent academics and institutional leaders, from a range of disciplines chosen from top universities worldwide—with a predominance of participation from the major universities in the English-speaking world. The natural sciences and the "hard" social sciences, such as economics, seem to be predominantly represented. Perhaps the largest numbers are senior administrators from top-tier universities—sitting or recently retired presidents, vice-chancellors, rectors, and the like. Few members seem to be from middle-ranking universities or emerging academic systems, and there are rarely members from universities within the country. An occasional business leader, often from the high-technology sector, is included. Seniority and maleness tend to predominate on the committees. From the university, members are often the senior management team—president, provost, vice presidents, and deans.

Advisory-committee members generally focus on service to overseas colleagues and assisting other universities. Many enjoy a bit of academic tourism, and some wish to learn some useful lessons from the university or committee colleagues. Few, if any, are able to devote a significant amount of time to the enterprise.

Do the Benefits Outweigh the Costs?

International-advisory committees, while not a major part of any university's budget, entail considerable costs. While the members typically serve without significant remuneration—with some exceptions—expenses are not inconsequential. Direct costs usually include business-class air transportation and related travel, and hospitality while on campus. Indirect costs, often not considered carefully, are not negligible—including the time of members in the entire senior management team of the university during the meetings, considerable preparation time mainly by the president and senior staff, and logistical arrangements. A two-day international-advisory committee meeting might cost well over US$100,000.

Characteristics of an Effective Committee

Members must not only be committed to the university but also require being knowledgeable about the institution and its challenges. Thus, they must be provided in advance with appropriate documentation and be committed to preparing well before arriving to the actual meeting. An advantage of the committee is a continuing relationship with the university, and thus trust and insights are built up over time. Committee members need some hands-on experience at the host institution—through conversations with professors, students, and other key stakeholders plus interactions with top management.

The topics discussed at committee meetings must be relevant and within the purview of expertise of the members. These policies might involve long- and medium-term institutional strategy, proposed polices relating to governance, the academic profession, new curriculum plans, internationalization, and other macro issues. Detailed administrative actions, specific personnel policies—the promotion of academics for example—and other detailed management and academic decisions are not the purview of advisory committees—although policies concerning promotion and evaluation of academics might be.

The meetings themselves must be carefully prepared, with sufficient time allocated for themes so that the discussion can be effectively organized. Lengthy presentations by university administrators must be avoided. A good balance between providing information on the one hand and allowing for in-depth discussion on the other is of basic significance.

While the size of the university group that participates in the meeting must be small enough to permit productive discussions, the advisory board's contribution can be more useful, along with a wider representation from the academic community. Senior faculty members and also junior colleagues, as well, may constructively be included in meetings. It is relevant that the discussions remain confidential, so the careful choice of local membership is important.

The university must be willing to expose problems and even crises, as well as to present good news and accomplishments. The advisory committee should not be considered as a rubber-stamping group but must be seen as part of the academic community.

Unlike a formal university board of trustees or governors, which exercises statutory supervisory responsibilities that sometimes place university leaders and board members in an antagonistic relationship, a major benefit of an international advisory board is that it can provide a nonthreatening platform for candid feedback on the host university's performance and for sharing relevant experiences to inform the university's strategy and new projects.

Conclusion

Distinguished outsiders can bring an original perspective, help raise awareness about new challenges, provide relevant advice based on long experience from a range of institutions, and perhaps present innovative approaches derived from international good practices. Dialogue between the university community and knowledgeable and sympathetic outsiders can yield useful insights. Moreover, there is nothing wrong with the added prestige of an international advisory committee.

[*IHE* 67, Spring 2012]

7

The Perils of Commercialism: Australia's Example*

More than two decades ago, the Australian government decided that international higher education should become an industry; since then it has become a major income producer for the nation. The higher education sector was motivated to make money from international education by government budget cuts—with revenue to be made up largely by entrepreneurial international activity. The result has been that, notwithstanding a further widespread and welcome internationalization of both student and staff profiles and important initiatives to internationalize programs, the prime goal of internationalization has become moneymaking (largely driven by government underfunding).

Government Pressure
Encouraged by government policies to marketize higher education and pushed to substitute fees from international students for declining state support, the higher education sector responded energetically with a wide range of initiatives. International student enrollments at Australian universities ballooned, as did income derived from their high tuition fees. Universities also developed a variety of overseas strategies, including branch campuses (in Vietnam, South Africa, Singapore, and elsewhere), twinning arrangements with educational institutions and business enterprises of various kinds in Malaysia and elsewhere. The Royal Melbourne Institute of Technology's Vietnam campus aims to have 10,000 enroll-

---

* With Anthony Welch

ments by 2012 and already has more than 120 international enrollments. Monash University's campus in Malaysia is already offering full medical degrees and has a current total enrollment of over 4,000, with 400 staff. Of the total growth in international student numbers, offshore enrollments have been the fastest-growing component.

The government cooperated by providing some funding for international outreach and, most significantly, by easing visa and other immigration regulations. Thus, this policy made it easy for international students to study in Australia and then remain in the country and work after completing their degrees and certificates.

Emerging Problems
From a financial perspective, the policy created huge success. Educational services became one of Australia's top exports, with official estimates of current total earnings from international education at around US$15.5 billion (most of which is from higher education). But, from an academic viewpoint, problems soon entered the system. Overseas, questions were raised about the quality and ethics of Australian institutional transplants. South Africa wondered about its Monash campus, while the Vietnam and Malaysian initiatives, which had strong support from their respective governments, were more successful. A few initiatives failed, such as the University of New South Wales in Singapore, costing the university many millions when it withdrew after failing to attract enough students.

Bottom-feeders entered the market, as usually happens when financial gain becomes the central motivator for international higher education. In the private sector, small vocational colleges in fields such as hairdressing and cooking attracted significant numbers of students from abroad, especially from South Asia, with promises of quick certificates and (sometimes spurious) jobs thereafter. Students with marginal qualifications began to stream in, some duped by exaggerated promises made by wily education agents in India. Outbreaks of anti–South Asian prejudice, in Melbourne and elsewhere, highlighting security problems of international students, created a firestorm of criticism in India, some of it sensationalized. While a recent survey of 1,600 international students from 10 universities showed that they still believed Australia to be the safest place to study—including alternative destinations such as the United States, United Kingdom, New Zealand, and Canada—the problem of attacks on international students was exacerbated by poor handling on the part of both police and politicians, each of whom attempted to label the attacks as opportunistic, rather than racist. The Australian Institute of Criminology has since announced a project to investigate the extent and forms of attacks on international students.

Additional problems arose. The Royal Melbourne Institute of Technology, one of the country's most active international universities, has just been accused of encouraging students to cheat on examinations. Press reports about international students being awarded degrees, despite showing up to exams drunk, and to exam papers being leaked to international students are part of an as yet unreleased Ombudsman Report, to which the university will be allowed to respond, before being tabled in the State of Victoria parliament. Previous cases have included allegations of plagiarism, directed at international students enrolled at the University of New England, via a commercial provider.

Such breaches of academic standards are the predictable results of more than a decade of underfunding of higher education, as a university president recently outlined: "The investment by the federal government fell by about 30 percent (per) student in real terms between 1996 and 2004." Indeed, while *Education at a Glance 2007* data reveal that on average public funding to higher education rose by 49 percent across the member countries of the Organization for Economic Cooperation and Development over the decade from 1995 to 2004, in Australia funding actually fell by 4 percent (the only member country where this occurred). Until funding is restored to previous levels—something the current federal government has promised to move toward—including a welcome promise to fund the real costs of research, institutions will continue to suffer and resort to internationalization as a budgetary strategy, rather than a cultural and learning strategy.

New Developments

Recent moves by the federal Department of Immigration to reduce the incentive for international students to enroll in short or poor-quality courses, with an eye on migration prospects, are having a welcome shake-out effect, with a number of weaker private vocational colleges that were too dependent upon international student fees having already collapsed. A revised list of occupations that accords priority to the highly skilled who have a job offer will certainly reduce the proportion of international students who cited the prospect of migration as a reason for studying in Australia, a rate that had risen from 5 percent in 2005 to a startling 24 percent by 2009. Current estimates are that international student numbers in Australia may fall by 20 percent, albeit mainly in the vocational sector, with a concomitant decline in revenues. However, for some universities that had grown too dependent upon high proportions of international enrollments, the effects are likely to be significant. Hopefully, the recently announced reforms will to some extent restore Australia's enviable international academic image—its "brand," which has already been significantly damaged. All of this is a predictable outcome of commercialism shaping international education. Australia's example has important lessons for other countries. The United Kingdom, for example, has not merely been pursuing similar policies, but the recently announced major budget cuts to universities will only push institutions there to pursue international student income even more vigorously.

[*IHE* 62, Winter 2011)

8

Reforming Higher Education in the Middle East—and Elsewhere

Among the rallying cries of the youthful revolutionary movements in the Middle East is a demand to reform higher education. The complaints are numerous and well founded. They include political interference at many levels, overcrowded classrooms, an inefficient and unresponsive administration, a decline in quality at all levels, an irrelevant curriculum, underqualified professors, and perhaps most significantly—degrees that do not lead to jobs.

Problems

The problem is that most of these demands cannot easily be met, regardless of the goodwill of new government and academic authorities or of a strong commitment to academic change. The crisis of Middle East higher education is systemic and requires an entire reconsideration of national higher education strategy. Resources, human and financial, are needed to a scale that is not practical to provide, at least in the short and probably the medium term.

At play are several fundamental issues that are not unique to the Middle East. The first is the inevitable massification of higher education. In the past several decades, every Middle Eastern country has not only experienced an explosion of the youth population but also an expansion in the numbers of young people attending universities. An additional phenomenon, common to many developing countries including the Middle East, is that higher education expansion has outstripped the ability of the economy to absorb university graduates. It is simply easier to expand enrollments than it is to provide jobs. Also, governments have the further incentive to "park" young people in universities for a while, rather than have them immediately join the ranks of the unemployed. A final issue is the deterioration of the average quality of higher education in the mass systems. Again, it is not surprising that, in the context of a mass system generally unaccompanied by concomitant increases in funding, greatly expanded enrollments result in diminished quality. Not only are students literally unable to find room in classes, but also their teachers often have no more than bachelor's degrees themselves.

What Can Be Done Now?

There are few "quick fixes" to deeply flawed higher education systems. One of these already being carried out in Egypt is depoliticizing the universities. Students demanded the removal of political appointments of administrators, controls over student elections, surveillance of students, and the other elements of the police state that pervaded Egyptian campuses; and to a considerable extent this trend has been accomplished

It may be possible to enhance administrative efficiency by emphasizing sound academic values and installing officials committed to the improvement of the universities. Corruption can be rooted out. Publicly emphasizing that the universities are now committed to academic values, excellence, and quality improvement may help boost morale, although this plan is not enough.

The Long Road Ahead

Unfortunately, real change is harder and requires both resources, as well, as a roadmap. Neither of these policies are easy to mobilize. Resources without policy produce waste. Creating practical higher education policy for any Middle East country is difficult to accomplish.

The reality of mass higher education is universal. As Egypt has shown, it is not enough to expand existing universities to enrollments of 200,000 or more students and to create new mass universities without clear missions or any semblance of appropriate resources. Parts of a program for reform and improvement include an appropriate mix of higher education institutions with differentiated missions, perhaps dismantling some of the mega-universities into smaller institutions, harnessing the growing but inadequately regulated private higher education to serve the public interest, and encouraging academics to obtain higher qualifications and paying them adequately.

Egypt, because of its large population and dependence on human resources for its future, also needs to have at least one world-class research university that can compete internationally, produce relevant research, and provide educated PhDs for the local market.

Other Middle East countries will have somewhat different circumstances and needs, but all face rather similar challenges.

The Dilemmas

Implementing reform is a challenge. One of the main problems concerns funding. For countries like Egypt and Tunisia, which have traditions of free or low-cost public higher education, charging meaningful tuition at the public universities is tremendously controversial and perhaps politically impossible in the atmosphere. Yet, this strategy is, perhaps unfortunately necessary, for it is impossible, except perhaps in Saudi Arabia and a few oil-rich Gulf countries, to have free-public higher education. Thus, ways will need to be found to introduce tuition fees, perhaps combined with appropriate loan and grant funds. There are simply insufficient public resources to support a quality mass higher education system.

The improvement of higher education in the Middle East includes upgrading the academic profession and providing an academic culture that promotes productivity. With a few notable exceptions, the quality of both teaching and research in the region is not high. Relatively few academics hold doctorates. With the exception of Saudi Arabia and a few Gulf countries, academic salaries are quite low. Academics have been kept down by the bureaucratic rules of the civil service, inadequate salaries, high teaching loads, and political repression—a powerful combination of negative forces. Ways will need to be found to build a creative academic culture and provide an academic environment so that the "best and brightest" will be attracted to teach and do research. Part of the problem will necessitate creating an academic system that rewards teaching and service in the majority of universities that accomplish little research.

Good governance also forms a necessary ingredient for any effective university. Academics must not only be well educated and reasonably paid, but they must have a role in the governance of the university. This process will be especially difficult to implement in the Middle East, where a combination of political control and a bureaucratic culture have stifled universities for decades. The demands of students to fully participate in governance are strong in the current environment, and students do have an appropriate role as members of the academic community. Experience shows, however, that the most successful universities are largely governed by the professoriate. Universities also need management, and professional administrators play an indispensable role. Thus, the most-effective universities are complex institutions that require significant autonomy in a broader context of accountability to the public.

The final dilemma is one of the most difficult ones—the relationship between the university to the employment market. Even well-qualified graduates cannot be guaranteed jobs if the economy is stagnating. Unemployed university graduates are a potent political force in many countries, and it is difficult to match the output of graduates to the available employment opportunities. The best reforms the educational system can do is to ensure the education of well-qualified graduates.

No doubt, the deficiencies of the higher education system contribute to political instability in the Middle East. Clearly, a significant reform is mandatory. Achieving needed reform in difficult political, social, and economic circumstances constitutes a daunting challenge. First, a roadmap for change is needed. Then, a social consensus must emerge to implement it.

[*IHE* 64, Summer 2011]

9

The "Subprime" Market and International Higher Education

It may be illuminating to compare the current subprime mortgage and housing-sector crisis in the United States and developments in international higher education. First, buyers and the housing and financial industries wanted to participate in a growing and lucrative housing market, just as many groups in the higher education industry now want to be players in international higher education. Housing prices were rising fast, and not many questions were asked about products, sellers, or buyers. This market was allowed to function without constraint. Then, a certain "irrational exuberance" set in, with the market becoming saturated and many speculators entering—in a way, a "bubble" mentality. Some buyers wanted to make a quick profit while others failed to recognize the risks of the new loans. Financial institutions got caught up and invented ever more complicated loan structures to spread risk globally. There was soon a growing recognition of the problems with the overheated housing and mortgage markets—inadequate supervision, oversupply of products, unsustainable costs, unfulfillable promises, and other challenges. In the mortgage/housing environment, the bubble has burst and many countries face very serious economic and social consequences. It is also noteworthy that the mortgage and housing crisis started in the largest market, the United States, and is spreading worldwide.

International higher education stands somewhere in the middle of the cycle—somewhere between irrational exuberance and a bubble. Now is the time to look at what actions are sustainable and what are not, what policy will serve the interests of students and the academic community, and what actions constitute mistaken policy or simple greed.

The academic community is committed to internationalization, although motivations differ and some institutions have no clear idea why they are involved. A recent survey by the International Association of Universities of academic leaders worldwide shows a huge variation of motivations, ranging from more internationally oriented students and staff, curricular improvement, building a "name brand," global collaboration, providing opportunities for research, and many others. Curiously, only a small minority of academic leaders cited earning income from international initiatives—an especially surprising point of view given that the Australian and British governments have emphasized earning money as a key goal of internationalization. University presidents, vice chancellors, and rectors from Europe and North America have been trooping to China and India prospecting for international business—such as, branch campuses, collaborative linkages, and joint-degree arrangements.

The Landscape
We know a few things about the international higher education landscape. There are perhaps 3 million students studying outside their own countries—with the largest number from Asia—with the largest number matriculating in the major English-speaking academic powers. An Australian study estimated that there will be 8 million international students by 2025, since cross-border study continues to be big business. No one knows how many branch campuses exist, but estimates are in the many hundreds—almost all of them located in developing or middle-income countries. The growth of "American University of . . . (fill in the blank)" is rapid as well. In addition to old and respected American-linked universities in Cairo and Beirut, institutions using the term "American" and often teaching in English are proliferating throughout the developing world, joined recently by institutions with "German," "French," or "Canadian" in their names. The expansion of academic offerings in English worldwide has created a new market for programs and for professorial mobility. The global higher education marketplace is large, growing, and basically unregulated. It is indeed the "Wild West" or, more appropriately, the "Wild East."

The Problems
In higher education, one might take the view that "the market will sort itself out" and thus leave hands off. Here again the subprime mortgage crisis represents a certain analogy regarding higher education.

By permitting unscrupulous players to perform and by encouraging more respectable banks to buy up risky debt without much regulation or restriction, the world has reached today's crisis. The financial instruments being used are very complex, and institutions worldwide have purchased them, reducing whatever accountability might have previously existed.

There is a similar mentality in the world of international higher education. Everyone can get into the market for international higher education. Sellers, including academic institutions and for-profit education providers, can easily enter the global market by selling educational products and services in a largely unregulated marketplace. Some of the sellers are prestigious universities hoping to build links overseas, recruit top students to their home campuses, and strengthen their name brands in the world market. Many of the sellers are themselves subprime institutions—sleazy recruiters, degree packagers, low-end private institutions seeking to stave off bankruptcy through the export market and even a few respectable universities forced by government funding cutbacks to enter foreign markets for profit making.

Buyers, such as students but also including some academic institutions in developing countries, are similarly unregulated, sometimes ill-informed and often naive. Most tragically, students and their families buy international educational services without much information or understanding. Sometimes recruited to study abroad at subprime schools or motivated more by the desire to seek employment than to study, students may be shortchanged. Uninformed or simply avaricious institutions in developing countries may partner with low-quality colleges and universities in, for example, the United States, Australia, the United Kingdom and receive substandard teaching or degree courses. Regulatory agencies may be entirely missing or inappropriate, thus making quality assurance impossible to achieve. There are not enough top-quality universities in countries like China and India to absorb all of the potential overseas partners. Further, most academic institutions worldwide lack the infrastructures to successfully engage in sophisticated international programs and initiatives.

How to Avoid a Crisis
Transparency is a key step for building a healthy international higher education environment. This approach means obtaining accurate information about the scope and extent of international higher education—by governments, international and regional organizations, and by universities. Information about motives and policies would also be useful, although now very little reliable information is available. The

market should not be left to determine the success or failure of international higher education. Some interests, especially the governments of the major "sellers" (such as the United States, Australia, and the United Kingdom and the for-profit education industry) argue that the doors to international commerce in higher education should be open and that this openness should be legislated by the World Trade Organization through the General Agreement on Trade in Services. Such forced openness would leave the world subject to whatever irrational exuberance and bubble mentality that is now evident in the mortgage industry and is increasingly in higher education.

The world also needs clear regulation, probably by government authority, to ensure that national interests are served and students and their families are not subjected to shoddy business practices by unscrupulous education providers. This will also help academic institutions themselves think about their motivations for entry into the global education market. Internationalization, including student mobility, cross-border educational provision, and involvement in the global knowledge economy of the 21st century is a positive and inevitable element of global higher education. What academe needs to avoid is succumbing to subprime practices and the inevitable crisis that will ensue.

[*IHE*, 51, Spring 2008]

10

Brain Drain or Brain Exchange?

The rich world is worrying about skills shortages, especially at the upper levels of their economies. The causes are many—such as a "demographic cliff" in Japan and in some European countries, significantly reducing the numbers of university-age young people, especially too few students enrolling in science, technology, engineering, and mathematics (STEM) fields, a leveling off of access, and low-degree completion rates. What is a solution of these problems? Increasingly, it is to boost the "stay rates" of international students—in other words, to convince international students, mainly from developing and middle-income countries, to remain after they complete their degrees. To oversimplify, the rich are robbing the brains of the developing countries—or for that matter any qualified brains who can be lured. Although the brain drain has been part of academia for a century or more, the situation is increasingly acute for all sides. For developing and emerging countries, the danger is that they will be left behind in the global knowledge economy, thus permanently damaging their futures.

Current Realities

In the era of globalization, it may be a bit of an exaggeration to call this a deliberate policy to encourage brain drain, but only slightly. Stay rates are already quite high. For example, 80 percent or more of Chinese and Indians who have obtained their advanced degrees in the United States over almost a half-century have remained in the country. It is hardly an exaggeration to point out that a significant part of Silicon Valley has been built with Indian brainpower. A recent analysis of data from the National Science Foundation's Survey of Earned Doctorates shows that the large majority of doctoral recipients from developing countries plan to remain in the United States, contributing to the academic labor force, particularly in the STEM fields. While data are seldom available, other European countries and Australia no doubt show similar trends. However, return rates are modestly increasing globally as developing country economies improve, and some of the rich world remains mired in recession.

Subsidies from the Poor to the Rich

Emerging and developing economies are actually contributing significantly to the academic systems of wealthier countries. International students contribute significantly to the economies of Europe, North America, and Australia while they are studying as well as if they remain. Data from 2011 indicate that the 764,000 international students studying in the United States contribute more than US$22 billion to the American economy annually. Similar statistics can be cited for the other major host countries. Indeed, Australia, which earns US$17 billion from international scholars, and the United Kingdom, where higher education is a US$21 billion earner, have both clearly stated national policies to increase income from overseas students.

Perhaps of greater concern are the subsidies provided by emerging and developing economies—through their doctoral graduates—who remain and join the academic profession in the rich countries. Here are examples from India and China—the two largest "brain exporters" in the world. It should be noted that these statistics are suggestive since details are unavailable and data points vary. In 2012, 100,000 Indian students were studying in the United States, mostly at the postbaccalaureate level. The large majority of these students remain after earning their degrees, and many join the local professoriate. Using UNESCO statistics, a rough estimate is that it costs the Indian taxpayer around US$7,600 in purchasing power parity (PPP) to educate a student from primary schooling through a bachelor's degree. It can be estimated that an Indian family may invest a similar amount in the education of a child—particularly since many of the young people who qualify for admission to overseas universities have been educated in private English-medium schools in India—for a total estimate of US$15,000. Thus, the approximate Indian investment in America, by paying for the education of 100,000 young people through the bachelor's degree, is approximately US$1.5 billion annually. The China figures are likely even higher. Although public expenditures on education are not available, research shows the average Chinese family invests US$39,000 PPP dollars to educate a student from primary through the completion of a bachelor's degree. There were 194,000 students from China studying in the United States in 2012. One can estimate that Chinese families were investing US$7.6 billion in brainpower in the United States. Significant additional funding from Chinese state sources were also being invested, although figures are unavailable.

It seems possible to approximate the educational contributions of the various, mostly developing, countries—whose young people are studying abroad—to the economies of the host countries. While not all of these students will remain after completing their studies, the sums are significant.

In addition to direct costs, the host countries benefit from an immense amount of intellectual capital from some of the brightest young people from the developing world. At the same time, the losses for developing countries are huge—for academe in particular, in research and teaching talent, new and innovative ideas that might have been cultivated from overseas experience, practices in university management, and many others.

Rich Country Strategies
Hans de Wit and Nannette Ripmeester provide an excellent summary of some of the policies aimed at increasing "stay rates" through changes in immigration policy, the provision of scholarships, closer links between universities and employers, and others (*University World News*, February 17, 2013). There is wide agreement in Europe and North America that new initiatives to entice the "best and brightest" of professionals from other countries, whom they educate, to stay and join the local labor force are a good idea. Efforts to liberalize visa regulations; open employment opportunities; permit postgraduate work, easier degree recognition; improvement of cooperation between the universities, governments, and industry; and many other initiatives are being implemented.

Countries, such as the United Kingdom and Australia, that recently implemented more stringent immigration limits, are rethinking their policies. The US National Academy of Sciences as well as universities advocate liberalizing visa regimes, in order to make it easier for foreign graduates to remain and work in the United States. There is absolutely no recognition of any contradiction between, for example, Millennium Development Goals, which stress the necessity for educational development in the emerging nations and policies aimed at attracting the best brains from developing countries.

African countries as South Africa and Botswana, which have relatively advanced higher education systems and pay more attractive salaries, also lure talent from elsewhere in Africa. Further, the academic brain drain operates between the major "academic powers," as well. Germany tries hard to attract back its postdocs and doctoral graduates, working in the United States, back to Germany, with only limited success. The attraction of a more stable academic career structure and somewhat higher salaries in the United States are attractive, and American universities try to keep the brightest international graduates, whatever their nationality.

The Complexities of a Globalized World

While location still matters and the world is by no means flat when it comes to academic excellence and power, globalization has certainly impacted universities and academic systems worldwide. The Internet has made communication and collaboration much easier. The proportion of research and publication conducted jointly by academics in more than one country has grown dramatically at the top of the system. Distance education, joint-degree programs, and branch campuses exhibit another aspect of a globalized academic world. None of this, however, makes up for losses in personnel.

China, as a country with large numbers of its academics working overseas, has instituted a number of programs to lure top Chinese researchers back to China. Joint appointments have also been offered for academics in key fields, so that Chinese universities can benefit from top scholars who wish to remain abroad. Other developing and middle-income countries also seek to leverage the academic diaspora through encouraging joint research projects, attracting investment, sponsoring academic organizations, and others. Successful programs have at least ensured that top local talent can benefit from expertise from compatriots who live abroad. Countries such as South Korea, Turkey, Scotland and others have implemented programs.

In all of these cases, however, the advantage remains with the major global academic centers for obvious reasons. Also, location matters a great deal; being part of an academic community is a much more powerful draw, even than Internet-based communication or sabbaticals or summers abroad. Stable academic careers, attractive salaries, academic freedom, unfettered access to the latest scientific and intellectual ideas, among other things, are a tremendous attraction. Few programs to bring back researchers and academics or efforts to limit academic mobility have been very successful. The fact is that until universities in developing countries offer the academic culture and facilities that top academics expect—including academic freedom, unrestricted information access, and laboratories—they will be unable to attract and retain top academic talent, but the policies of the rich countries certainly do not help.

Academic Justice?

Do the "academic powers" have any responsibility to developing academic systems? A sense of responsibility for encouraging doctoral graduates from the developing world to return home, to build universities, and to improve the quality of emerging academic systems is entirely absent from the current discussion. The only concern is to improve "stay rates" and liberalize immigration rules to ensure that the maximum number of the best and brightest from the developing world remains. Should the rich world at the least, in the context of Millennium Development Goals, remit to the developing world the costs incurred, by developing countries, in educating their nonreturning young people? There are many ways to at least ameliorate the situation—for example, joint doctoral degrees that provide young developing country scholars an opportunity to study abroad for part of their PhD work, while retaining a link to their home university and at the same time building research capacity. Then, at least, the developing countries would not be directly subsidizing the academic systems of the rich.

[*IHE* 72, Summer 2013]

11

The Complexities of 21st-Century Brain Exchange

The emerging economies of the BRICs (Brazil, Russia, India, and China) will, it is assumed, lure both home students who go abroad to study when they finish their degrees and some graduates who have settled in the West—because of their dramatic economic growth and expanding higher education systems. The problem is that data seem to show that this is not the case. The brain drain, now euphemistically called the brain exchange, seems to be alive and well. Research by Dongbin Kim, Charles A. S. Bankart, and Laura Isdell ("International doctorates: Trends analysis on their decision to stay in US," *Higher Education* 62, August 2011) shows that the large majority of international doctoral recipients from American universities remain in the United States after graduation. Even more surprisingly, the proportion of those choosing to stay in the United States has increased over the past three decades, seemingly regardless of growth and academic expansion. There is strong evidence that we live in a worldwide era of global mobility of highly skilled talent in general and of the academic profession in particular, but this mobility flows largely in one direction—from developing and emerging economies to the wealthier nations, especially to the English-speaking countries.

Much has been written about the supposedly obsolescence of the term brain drain. Globalization, it is argued, brings in its train a globally mobile and highly educated labor force—creating a kind of brain exchange among countries. But the data reported here show that mobility, while quite sizable, is one-way, mainly from developing and emerging economies to wealthier nations. There is a growing flow of ideas and capital back to countries of origin, but one cannot escape the fact that the major economic and social contribution is made in the country in which an individual is primarily located. The realities of globalization remain highly unequal. While brains may no longer be permanently drained, they are nonetheless siphoned, with the possibility (not that frequently implemented) of returning to their origins.

Who Goes and Who Stays?

The countries with the most impressive economic and educational expansion seem to be those with the largest "stay" rates, according to the National Academy of Science's Survey of Earned Doctorates (SED), which tracks all international doctoral students studying in the United States. For example, during the 1980s, 25.9 percent of Chinese doctoral graduates returned immediately after completing their degrees. In the 2000s, the return percentage had declined to 7.4 percent. India's figures are also quite low—13.1 percent returned in the 1980s and 10.3 percent in the 2000s. Yet, return rates vary considerably, ranging from 84 percent of Thais, 60 percent of Mexicans and Brazilians, and 39.5 percent of Africans. A particular surprise is the European return rate, which has gone from 36.9 to 25.7 percent over 30 years.

There are other variables, as well. Women are somewhat more likely to remain in the United States than men. International students who have their bachelor's degree in the United States are also more likely to stay, as are students who come from well-educated families. Field of study also seems to make a difference, with degree holders in agriculture (54.2%), education (48.5%), and social science (44.1%) most likely to return, and those in biology (19.3%), physical science (21.8%), and business (31.9%) less likely.

The SED data exhibit some limitations. Students typically complete a questionnaire asking for background information, educational experience, and plans supplied by the National Science Foundation and administered by graduate schools nationwide when they submit their approved doctoral dissertation. Some respondents may not be fully aware of their plans. Furthermore, plans reported in the SED may not work out. Some students may, for example, obtain a postdoc and return home after that for a variety of reasons. Others may, in the current difficult academic job market, unsuccessfully search for a position. Because the SED measures only doctoral completion, it is likely that this group is mainly headed for academic jobs—we know nothing about return rates for MBA holders or those completing bachelor's or master's degrees. Despite limitations, the SED is the most accurate tool available.

The study-abroad statistics cited here relate only to the United States, but it is quite likely that the general pattern of mobility is similar for other host countries and, especially, the major English-speaking and large continental European nations. Variations based on immigration policies, local labor markets, the relatively openness of the academic system and economy, language, and other factors will no doubt affect stay rates.

Patterns and Policies

Some economies and academic systems have benefited substantially from the patterns noted here. For example, an estimated one-quarter of Silicon Valley high-technology start-ups were established by immigrants, many of whom received their advanced education in the United States. American universities, from the most prestigious institutions to community colleges, have large numbers of immigrant scholars and scientists on their faculties, and a growing number have risen to top leadership positions.

Why do the international doctoral holders, counted by the SED, choose to remain in the United States? While each case has an individual story, the general reasons are not hard to determine. For all of the current problems of American colleges and universities, the terms and conditions of academic work—including salaries—are by international standards quite good. Having studied in the United States, international degree holders have familiarity with the system and often can call on mentors to assist them in the local job market. Although a few countries, such as China, offer incentives for top graduates to return home, such programs are small and serve only the top elite. For many, returning home to academic institutions that may be hierarchical and sometimes ill-equipped is not an attractive prospect. In the emerging economies, academic salaries are low and moonlighting is often necessary to support a middle-class lifestyle. Even in China's top universities, which have received massive infusions of money and have built impressive campuses, the academic culture is often problematical for graduates familiar with the relatively open and meritocratic institutions in the United States or other better-established academic systems. While conditions and salaries may be better in the emerging high-tech and business sectors in the emerging economies, problems persist. Efforts by countries—such as, China and India—to lure their graduates home have been mostly unsuccessful. Some European nations, including Germany, have also actively tried to entice their PhDs and postdocs to return, with only modest success.

The immigration policies of the rich countries also play a central role. Despite America's success in retaining its international doctoral graduates, US immigration policy until quite recently has not been aimed at easing entry to the highly skilled. Even now greater emphasis is placed on uniting families, increasing the diversity of the immigrant population, and other factors. It remains to be seen whether pressure from the high-tech community and others will be adopted to open opportunities to the highly skilled. Other countries, including Canada and Australia, have quite consciously tailored immigration policy to favor highly educated groups and have made it easy for international graduates to remain in the country and build a career. European countries are also moving in this direction.

Conclusion

The statistics reported here may come as a surprise to some observers. These data are likely an inevitable result of globalization and the inequalities in higher education and in wealth and development that persist. It is fair to say that the host countries are unconcerned about these imbalances, and indeed most are moving to strengthen their advantages through adjustments in academic and scholarship policies and immigration regulations. If stay rates are a sign of continuing inequalities in the global knowledge system and in higher education, it will demand achieving a better balance and will require time, resources, and in some cases, changing in academic structures and practices. While there is much rhetoric about globalization creating a "level playing field," the realities show something quite different.

[*IHE* 68, Summer 2012]

12

Another Week, Another Scandal: Immigration Dilemmas and Political Confusion*

Immigration regulations for international students seem to be changing somewhat unpredictably of late, in major receiving countries. In several English-speaking nations, immigration regulation has become a significant policy issue, and international students are the frequent focus of recent crackdowns. These changes have the potential for altering the landscape of global student flows and might even slow the increases in student numbers of the past two decades. In this context, the expansion of recent years might actually have been a temporary "bubble."

Recent Scandals
The latest crisis involved London Metropolitan University (LMU), an institution with one of the largest enrollments of international students in the United Kingdom. The UK Border Authority withdrew its "highly trusted sponsor" status from the university, after an audit revealed that a significant number of international students did not have appropriate or adequate documentation to remain in the United Kingdom, adequate English-language skills, or had not registered for classes. Some of these students may need to return to their home countries. Other international students, legitimately enrolled, are panicked. A large percentage of London Metropolitan University's

---

With Liz Reisberg

international students come from India. As explained by the manager of a firm that places students at UK universities (quoted recently in the *Guardian* newspaper): "We divide the market into two categories: the university market for genuine students and the immigration market." The challenge for immigration authorities is how to distinguish the two groups, when both arrive with student visas. Many observers see the LMU case as the tip of the iceberg of questionable admissions and recruiting practices in the United Kingdom.

Scandals have made national headlines in the United States, as well. In August 2012, the head of Herguan University in California was arrested on charges of visa fraud. This follows the similar case of Tri-Valley University, and both serve mainly Indian students with little intention of studying. Both appear to have operated profitably as "visa mills." As neither institution is duly accredited, one has to wonder why these were authorized to issue student visas at all.

But there are different levels of misdeeds, and not all merit an immediate and draconian response. The US State Department caused mayhem last May after determining that 600 instructors, attached to Chinese government–sponsored Confucius Institutes, were inappropriately documented and would have to leave the country immediately and then reapply for visas in order to return. In this case there was no subterfuge, only a seemingly innocent misunderstanding of confusing visa regulations. In the end, no instructors were deported, but the way the State Department handled the incident came close to causing a major diplomatic tangle with the Chinese government.

Political Pressure and Political Response

It seems that there is a "perfect storm" of concern over the movement of individuals across borders. In North America, Europe, and Australia, the issue of immigration is increasingly present in political discourse. Perhaps reacting to job losses due to the economic recession and a general conservative trend in many countries, immigration has become a political "hot button." The United Kingdom, for example, has a policy goal to reduce immigration into the country. In many other European countries, immigration is politically sensitive, often used by populists on the extreme right as a central and provocative theme. Many US states have made illegal immigration a political focus.

Australia seems to vacillate between wanting more and wanting less immigration. In a move earlier this year, graduating international students will now be allowed to remain to work for two to four years (up from a previous limit of 18 months) without any restrictions on the type of employment.

Malaysia wants more foreign students but recently introduced new restrictions to constrain the flow. The government now requires students to demonstrate that they have been accepted to a higher education institution before entering the country, also that international students study Bahasa Malaysia during their first year and that they buy medical insurance. These new measures are indicative of an international trend toward greater regulation.

More governments are concerned that the flow of international students needs more oversight and controls. In the past, academic institutions have been given considerable leeway over the admission of international students and the subsequent granting of study visas. Immigration authorities relied on academic institutions to ensure that only qualified, legitimate students are recommended for visas. Recent events indicate that a segment of educational institutions, typically those highly dependent on income from international students, may be taking advantage of their freedom as gatekeepers and not behaving "in the spirit of the law."

Protection for Whom?

International students are easy targets in this rarified environment. As a transient group they are not well-positioned to become a political force or to create a lobby to speak for them. But importantly, they are less of a threat than other temporary visitors. Unlike tourists who enter countries and are impossible to track afterwards, international students are registered at an educational institution and entered into immigration databases.

International students are also particularly vulnerable to exploitation. They are subject to confusing and changing laws that they can only barely comprehend, evidenced in the debacle with the instructors of the Confucius Institutes. These students and scholars are likely to accept (and often pay for!) advice from others, who may not have the student's best interest at heart. They are also less likely to know the rights and protection available to them in another country, raising concerns in Australia that the new work privileges will encourage unscrupulous employers to exploit this new class of foreign workers.

Much as governments need to protect visas programs from abuse, so students need to be protected from abusers.

The New Ethos

The landscape of international higher education has changed in recent years and this contributes to the necessity of screening students more carefully. Some academic institutions rely on international students to balance the budget. At these institutions, international students have become a "cash cow." Australia is the best example—with government policy for several decades encouraging earning revenue through international endeavors. While the United States has no national policy concerning international ventures, several states—notably, New York and Washington—have determined that income from international students should be an important part of a public institution's financial strategy. At some institutions, international students now represent the difference between enrollment shortfalls and survival, due to changing demographics in their traditional student market.

It is worth noting that some receiving countries welcome international students without the same degree of "commercialization." Canada, for example, while it does charge international students higher fees, permits highly skilled graduates from abroad to remain in the country after completing their studies. In the Canadian case, international students promise an influx of talent as well as additional revenue. Germany, Norway, and several other European countries do not charge fees to international students.

Internationalization has presented new opportunities for commercialization in countries where institutions have a long history of autonomy. Institutional leaders who represent a new ethos, more attentive to revenue than to educational integrity or quality, are free to subsume various dimensions of the academic enterprise—including admissions, student supervision, degree qualifications—to the bottom line.

This new ethos is evident where universities have outsourced overseas, recruiting to agents and recruiters who are paid commissions for delivering applications and enrolling international students. Of course, the introduction of third-party recruiter adds another level of interaction between the university and the student giving immigration authorities additional reason for concern about how students are screened for admission and visas.

Addressing the Problem

The general reaction from the academic community has been negative to the imposition of additional governmental restrictions concerning overseas students and other aspects of international higher education. Few people acknowledge the seriousness of the problem and express concern that stricter immigration policies will reduce international enrollments and contribute to an "unwelcoming" image overseas.

The problem is that immigration and border enforcement agencies tend to respond, by applying legal and bureaucratic rules that lack nuance. Considering that the majority of the millions of internationally mobile students are qualified for the programs, where they are enrolled, and that they contribute intellectually as well as economically to the institutions that host them, dramatic changes in immigration should be contemplated carefully. When individuals enter a country in violation of immigration regulations, they are (and should be) subjected to sanctions. When institutions ignore rules or admit unqualified students, they should be subjected to penalties or legal action. In some cases, they are closed down. This is inevitable.

In fact, governments do need to bring some additional discipline to the management of international higher education, particularly where financial interests may determine institutional policy and practice. But this needs to be done in a way that does not penalize everyone.

[*IHE* 70, Winter 2013]

13

Getting Graduates to Come Home —Not So Easy[*]

It is said that we live in the new era of the "brain exchange," but in our view the old-style brain drain continues to a significant degree. With only modest success, countries, such as China, continue to try to get some of their scholars who have stayed abroad after completing advanced degrees to return home. In fact the large majority of Chinese (and Indian) students who have gone abroad for study have not returned home over more than 20 years. Moreover, the numbers recently have only improved modestly despite China's impressive economic and academic growth.

Historically, governmental efforts to convince scholars to return home have not prevailed. India, for example, has over the years created a variety of programs to attract back successful Indian academics who settled abroad. One challenge is to match overseas salaries. Perhaps the most important serious issue—the academic conditions in Indian universities and laboratories are often problematical. Some academics who were lured by these special programs found working conditions and the academic culture inadequate and returned to their positions in the West. Only at the Indian Institutes of Technology and of Management has there been limited success.

The Chinese government and universities have also tried in many ways to convince scholars and scientists settled abroad to return, with only modest results. Similar programs in other countries have been similarly ineffectual.

With Wanhua Ma

China recently has started a program to lure scholars back home by providing significant financial and other incentives to Chinese PhDs working abroad. The program is named the 111 Project. The national 111 Project was introduced by the Ministry of Education and the State Administration of Foreign Expert Affairs, intending to invite 1,000 top scholars from the world top 100 universities to build 100 world-class innovation bases at top Chinese universities, in which top foreign-trained experts work with domestic experts to conduct high-level research, to enhance higher-level scientific competence and comprehensive competitive power globally. The program originated in 2005, and it created a lot of interest in China because it expressed a kind of urgency and eagerness in attracting some of the world's top Chinese scientists back home. Many universities have used this opportunity to establish research initiatives and centers. So far, 662 111 Project scientists have been selected, and 310 of them are now working at Chinese research universities.

Unanticipated Consequences
However, the program has created some unanticipated problems. Some Chinese universities do not fully understand the international academic labor market and, in their search for overseas talent, have relied on résumés, educational background, titles, personal contacts, and recommendations rather than on careful evaluations of prospective candidates and their academic work and impact. In some cases, the sponsoring universities found that the scholars and scientists who agreed to return are not the ones most desired. Those who decided to return may be late career professors from middle-ranking US and UK universities who, perhaps, see a stagnant career in the United States or United Kingdom and desire either a fresh start or a cushy job in China. Some use their newfound fame in China as a platform for pontificating on a range of topics. Top-ranking Chinese academics from the best Western universities generally have not been willing to return permanently. At best, they agree to some kind of joint affiliation with a top Chinese university and visit periodically to lecture, provide advice, and collaborate with professors in China. This policy may in fact be the best strategy for taking advantage of top overseas Chinese expertise.

Another unanticipated result of the program is salary compression—highly paid returnees earn much higher salaries than local academics, often creating envy and morale problems. The success of any academic department and this program involves the sense of academic community, which can be shattered by highly unequal salaries or better working conditions and facilities for the returnees. When domestic professors find that a returnee may not contribute more than they do, they may refuse to cooperate, and harm the work of the department. While many of the returned scholars can still speak Chinese, they may not understand the new academic culture in China. Lack of cooperation from local colleagues and problems of re-entry include the academic realities the returned scholars face.

Solutions

Using the talent of academics from developing and middle-income countries who have, for many reasons, chosen to settle in the West is a laudable goal. Yet, even in a globalized world, luring some of the top academics home is not an easy task, and most of the programs that have been attempted have failed. The truth is that as long as the conditions of academic work vary significantly from country to country—including salaries, conditions of academic work, the academic culture, and academic freedom, to name a few—the "best and brightest" are unlikely to return. Those who are most desirable—midcareer academics who are highly productive and located at the top universities—are the least likely to return.

The best that can be done—and it is in fact quite a good alternative—is to build ties with these academic "stars" and create ties that can yield practical results that will neither harm the local academic culture nor demand impractical results.

[*IHE* 63, Spring 2011]

14

Academic Salaries and Contracts: What Do We Know?*

Data in this article are from *Paying the Professoriate: A Global Comparison of Compensation and Contracts*, edited by Philip G. Altbach, Liz Reisberg, Maria Yudkevich, Gregory Androushchak, and Iván F. Pacheco (New York: Routlege, 2012). Additional data can be found on the project Web site: http://acarem.hse.ru. This research resulted from a collaboration between the Center for International Higher Education at Boston College and the Laboratory of Institutional Analysis at the National Research University–Higher School of Economics, Moscow, Russia.

Salaries and the terms of faculty appointments and promotion are central to the well-being of the academic profession and its contributions to the university. If salaries are inadequate, the "best and brightest" will not be attracted to academe, and those who do teach will be obliged to moonlight, diverting their attention and dedication from their academic work. Additionally, without appropriate contracts and appointments, there is a limited guarantee of academic freedom or expectation of either a stable or satisfying career. Furthermore, in a globalized world, salaries in one country affect academe elsewhere, as professors are tempted to move where remuneration and working conditions are best.

Yet, only limited research is available about these issues, within a specific country or comparatively. Comparative studies on academics in many countries are complex, as data are often difficult to obtain; and

* With Iván F. Pacheco

exchange rates and the standard of living vary across countries. The research provided data using purchasing power parity, which permits more realistic salary comparisons. The project reveals key trends in 28 diverse countries on all continents.

Salaries and Remuneration

This research, not surprisingly, found significant variations in academic salaries worldwide. As a general rule, salaries were best in wealthier countries, although there are significant variations among them, with the English-speaking academic systems generally paying more than those in continental Europe. Russia and the former Soviet countries pay quite low salaries, even when their economies are relatively prosperous. There were a few surprises. India ranks comparatively high in salaries. China, on the other hand, has invested heavily in its higher education system, particularly in its research universities; yet, average academic salaries rank at the bottom.

It was also learned that, in many countries, salary alone does not convey a complete picture of compensation. Academics also depend on other payments and subsidies, from their universities, and other sources—to make up the total remuneration package. Chinese universities, for example, provide a complex set of fringe benefits and extra payments to their academic staff for publishing articles, evaluating extra examinations, and for other campus work. In North America and western Europe, salaries are the main academic income—while elsewhere this does not seem to be the case.

In many countries, salaries are too low to support a middle-class lifestyle locally, and other income is needed. In many of these places, moonlighting is common. Many academics teach at more than one institution. Indeed, the burgeoning private higher education sector in many countries depends on professors from the public universities to teach most classes.

Contracts

The terms and conditions of academic appointments and subsequent opportunities for advancement available to the academic profession are also of central importance. Among the group of 28 countries, few offer formal tenure to the academic profession, thus perhaps weakening guarantees of academic freedom and providing less job security. Tenure arrangements, awarded to academics after a careful evaluation of performance, seem largely limited to the United States, Canada, Australia, the Netherlands, and South Africa in the study. In one country, Saudi Arabia, local academic staff receive permanent appointments, at the time of hiring. Some continental European countries provide civil service status to academics in the public universities, and this also provides significant job security. In fact, in most countries, few are fired and few are seriously evaluated. There is a kind of de facto tenure that provides long-term employment for most, without either a guarantee or any means of careful evaluation.

A number of important variations exist in requirements to enter the profession or (when available) to qualify for a tenured-like position. In many countries, a doctoral degree is requisite to become a university professor. In certain European countries (Czech Republic, France, Germany, and Russia) a habilitation—similar to a doctoral dissertation—is needed, in addition to the doctoral degree, to achieve the rank of professor. In other countries, a simple bachelor's degree is sufficient to be hired as a university teacher. In countries where a PhD is not required, there is a trend to demand higher qualifications; and the master's degree is becoming the minimum requirement, even if it is not mandatory by law.

International Mobility
Among the countries that pay the best salaries, some benefit based on an inflow of academics from less-wealthy countries. Australia, Canada, the Netherlands, Saudi Arabia, and the United States benefit the most from the migration of academic talent. In contrast, many of the countries paying the lowest salaries are considered "sender" countries and some (Armenia, Ethiopia, Israel, and Nigeria) have implemented programs, in which better salaries and working conditions are part of the strategy to attract or retain national and international scholars. In their quest to build world-class education systems, China and Saudi Arabia are aggressively pursuing international faculty, mostly from English-speaking countries, as well as their own expatriates. In the Chinese case, that process has resulted in a big gap between the salary of local professors and international/repatriated ones. Finally, some countries are both "senders" and "receivers." For example, South Africa attracts professors from other African nations, but at the same time it frequently suffers brain drain to English-speaking countries—such as, the United Kingdom, Australia, and the United States.

Conclusion
This research shows a range of realities for the academic profession. Some countries offer reasonable salaries and secure and transparent career structures for academics. The English-speaking countries included in this research—Canada, the United Kingdom, Australia, to

some extent South Africa, and the United States—fall into this category. Western European countries that offer civil service status to academics typically provide decent working conditions and compensation. But even in these nations, the professoriate is inadequately compensated when compared to other highly educated professionals. For the rest, and this includes Russia and the former Soviet Union, China, Latin America (except Brazil), and Nigeria, salaries are low and contracts often lack transparency. India offers reasonably good salaries.

A global comparison presents an array of realities—few of them extraordinarily attractive—for the professoriate. This situation, at least for the 28 countries examined in this research, is certainly problematical for countries at the center of the global knowledge economy. For academics in those countries with quite low salaries—such as, China, Russia, Armenia, or Ethiopia—the academic profession faces a crisis. In general, it seems like professors are not considered the elite in the knowledge economy. Rather, they tend to be seen as a part of the skilled labor force that such economies require.

[*IHE* 68, Summer 2012]

15

The Intricacies of Academic Remuneration

How can we comprehend academic salaries? Does the sum paid monthly to a professor constitute his or her full remuneration? Our research on international comparisons of academic salaries found major variations among countries. Differences exist as well within countries—by rank, discipline, and other factors. In some countries, salaries are determined by an individual's age, length of employment, rank, and often by civil service rules—without much cognizance of productivity or academic accomplishment. Indeed, in much of the world, academics are paid on the basis of their length of service and rank alone. In other countries, particularly in some of the newer private universities, salary structures are far from transparent.

The full-time professoriate—probably a global minority of the academic profession overall, since in many countries part-timers dominate the academic system—is divided by role, function, type of institution, and discipline. As interpreted by sociologist Burton Clark, the academic profession is divided by "small worlds, different worlds." Academics are also divided by salaries. In many countries, faculty in private universities earn more than their counterparts in public institutions. Our research shows significant variations by rank. Not surprisingly, in our study of 15 countries, senior professors earned on average significantly more than junior staff.

Patterns
Among most full-time academic staff in North America, western

Europe, much of Asia, and Australia, the salary paid by the university is the bulk of the total income earned. Relatively little extra income is earned through consulting, part-time teaching, or other sources. The salary, particularly if there are two income earners in the family, provides for an adequate if not lavish middle-class lifestyle commensurate with national standards. As our research shows, while academic salaries vary considerably, in the regions mentioned here, full-time academics can survive on their university incomes.

This is not the case in Latin America, most of Africa, or some of the countries of central and eastern Europe and the former Soviet Union. In these countries, full-time academic salaries generally do not provide sufficient income, and academics must earn additional money from other sources. Some hold more than one academic position, as the growing private higher education sector in many countries is staffed largely by "moonlighting" professors from the inadequately paid public universities. Others do consulting, own businesses, and a significant number do private tutoring or other activities that border on corrupt academic practices.

Some Academics Are Less Equal Than Others
In many countries, academic remuneration from the university is not equivalent to the base salary from the university. There are many reasons for this. Salaries are often nationally stipulated by government authorities or through union contracts or other arrangements. Universities may be unable to differentiate among disciplines, pay anything close to "market rates" to professors who are in high demand in the labor market, or reward highly productive scholars. Faculty members living in high-cost urban areas may earn the same as professors in lower-cost regions.

Most faculty members serve as teachers and possess few if any research expectations or accomplishments. In many parts of the world, particularly in developing countries, a large number of university teachers hold a bachelor's or master's degree and not a doctorate. For this large proportion of the academic profession, the base salary is the full income provided by the employing university, and in some countries additional income is needed. In others, the base salary is sufficient if not particularly attractive.

For Other Professors, More Is Required
For a relatively small minority of the academic profession, the standard salaries offered by most universities are insufficient to keep them in academe or, in some cases, even within their home country. These

academics are research-active faculty members found in all fields but larger numbers in the sciences than the humanities, mostly located at top universities, and in "hot" fields such as management, information technology, or biotechnology, where salaries outside the universities are very high. These academic "stars" form a modest proportion of the academic profession in any country, ranging possibly from 2 to 10 percent of the total professoriate. Indeed, without this group little research would be undertaken and universities would have no chance to succeed in the international rankings.

"Salary progression"—the difference in salary between junior and senior professors—in general appears modest compared to the situation in the professions outside academe. According to our research, for most of the 15 countries in the study, salaries seldom doubled between entry level and senior ranks. The major industrialized countries (including Germany, France, Canada, the United States, and the United Kingdom) stood at the bottom, in terms of variations between junior and senior ranks, and the developing countries (such as China, South Africa, Argentina, and others) at the top. India ranks poorly on both progression and on basic salary. The lack of possibilities for improved salaries is a problem for the profession in general, but it is particularly damaging for the most productive academics. The latter are the most likely to leave academe or to go to countries with higher salaries.

How are these academic highflyers paid in the bureaucratic and rather flat academic salary environment of academe? For a start, in a few countries and frequently in private higher education, salary structures are relatively flexible, and it is possible to pay top professors significantly higher direct salaries than the rank and file. American private universities are the most dramatic examples, where highly productive professors, those in fields such as law or management, and scholars holding endowed chairs may obtain salaries possibly double or more than other senior academics earn. In these institutions and in some others in the United States and elsewhere, universities are able to compensate professors based in part on market-rate salaries for fields and individuals in high demand.

Research-active professors often teach less—providing them more time to focus on research and thus compensating them with time instead of salary. It is common for professors to be directly paid by their universities for research production. In some places, professors are paid by their university or a government agency for each article they publish in a prestigious journal. Where professors are able to obtain research grants from external sources they are often paid a part of the grant income. Research-active faculty in some countries can be compensated by government agencies set up to boost incomes, often as members of organizations of researchers. The Mexican Sistema Nacional de Investigadores is an example.

While these and other arrangements create inequalities in compensation among professors and universities within an academic system, they are necessary to reward research-active faculty.

Salary Is Not Always Remuneration

For many reasons, the incomes earned by academics do not always coincide with the salary provided by the university. Universities sometimes try to boost compensation to meet high urban living costs and keep professors from leaving the institution for higher paying jobs elsewhere in the economy. Some institutions, as in the case of Makerere University in Uganda, have established extra academic programs for students to let professors earn extra income by teaching additional high-fee-paying students. Many academics earn extra money on their own by consulting, holding appointments in more than one university, or other schemes.

It is often difficult to measure nonsalary income. Universities have few ways of tracking income sources. Individual academics, particularly those with creative ways of boosting their incomes, have little incentive to report extra income. Nonsalary income provides, in the cases of research-active professors, a necessary way of rewarding highly productive faculty. Other extra-salary compensation supplements unrealistically low salaries. However, certain forms of such compensation may lead to corruption, unfair advantages, or other problems. Salaries frequently are insufficient to attract or retain the best scholars and scientists, and attractive remuneration is absolutely necessary to reward productive academics in a complex and globalized university.

[*IHE* 54, Winter 2009]

16

Academic Career Structures:
Bad Ideas*

Successful universities and academic systems require career structures for the academic profession that permit a stable academic career,
encourage the "best and brightest" to join the profession, reward the
most productive for their work, and weed out those who are unsuited
for academic work. We have been struck by the dysfunctional nature of
career structures in many countries—with disturbing negative trends—
and would, only with a small sense of irony, suggest a ranking for career
structures that guarantee to fail to build a productive academic profession. Our serious point is this: without a career structure that attracts
quality, rewards productivity, and permits stability, universities will
fail in their mission of high-quality teaching, innovative research, and
building a "world-class" reputation.

Taxicabs and Nontenure Track
A few examples will illustrate how poorly designed or badly implemented academic career structures can have a severely negative impact
on the profession—and ultimately on the future of higher education.
Many look to the United States as the world's leading university system
and to the American professoriate as highly productive. The US "up-or-
out" tenure system is seen as a rigorous but effective way of ensuring
careful selection while at the same time providing a clear career path.
While the system has been criticized for downplaying teaching and

* With Christine Musselin

sometimes imposing unrealistic time constraints on junior staff, it is widely seen as effective. The problem is that fewer than half of new academic appointments in the United States are made on the traditional "tenure stream"; most new appointments are either part-time or full-time contracts. While the situation is somewhat better at the top institutions, this new arrangement makes an academic career impossible for participants of this new system. While this policy may save money and increase flexibility in the short run, it will have a highly negative impact on the American academic profession. The first increasing difficulty involves attracting the most qualified individuals to academe and constrains young researchers while autonomy should be provided at an age when creativity and innovation are usually at the highest levels.

Argentina may come close to the top rank for irrationality and complexity. Although the large proportion of Argentine academics have low-paid part-time appointments (the original "taxicab professors"), the minority who have full-time appointments face a bizarre career path. If a faculty member wishes to be promoted to the highest academic rank, he or she must submit to a *"concours"* where the position occupied by the incumbent is open to applicants from all over the country or indeed the world. In other words, these academics are not promoted on the basis of their performance but may instead have to struggle for "their" job against other applicants. The only saving grace is that the system is often so inefficient that the *concours* is not organized and the incumbent is promoted anyway. Needless to say, the *concours* system produces immense stress among academics and deters many from entering the profession or from applying to proceed upward in the ranks.

European Anomalies

In France, the access to a first permanent position as *maître de conférences* occurs rather early compared with other countries (on average prior to the age of 33 years) and opens the path to 35 to 40 years of an academic career. These recruitments happen after a period of high uncertainty as in almost all disciplines the ratio of "open positions per doctors" has worsened, while the doctoral degree is still not recognized as a qualification by businesses or the public sector. Recruiting a new *maître de conférences* thus constitutes a high-stake decision making. But currently university departments have about two months to examine the candidates, select some of them, hold a 20- to 30-minute interview with those on the short list, and rank the best ones. Despite the highly selective process that the first candidate on the list successfully passes, this new colleague is rarely considered as a chance on which to build by the recruiting university. Not only is the salary based on a national bureaucratic scale below the average GDP per capita for France, but new academics are frequently not offered a personal office and may be asked to teach the classes colleagues do not want to offer or to accept administrative duties. The difficult road toward the doctorate leads to a rather disappointing and frequently non-well-remunerated situation, thus undermining the attractiveness of the career.

In Germany, the access to a stable career occurs much later than in France, at 42 on average for a first tenured position as professor. From the doctorate to the professorship, most young academics spend many years in the *Mittelbau*—as postdocs, research assistants, or other positions. Survivors of this long and uncertain period of apprenticeship become autonomous professors who negotiate the number of assistantships, thus replicating as professors what they experienced in the *Mittelbau*. For sound reasons, a 2002 reform was intended to oppose the negative consequences of the long period of apprenticeship and to increase the institutional control over professors. Merit-based salaries were thus introduced for all new professors. The resources they receive when they are recruited cover three to five years and are renegotiated according to their performance. However, most academics find the new income system less satisfactory than the former. On top of that, the reform creates quasi tenure-track positions for young scholars, who thus become more independent from senior professors.

It is too early to tell if these new positions will lead more easily to professorships as there are currently fewer than 800. This turnabout may discourage academics in the traditional *Mittelbau*, who still experience the control of professors but know that if they themselves become professors the long apprenticeship period may be undermined by an autonomous apprenticeship; professors would also face income conditions that are simultaneously less attractive.

Several European countries—including Germany, France, and Russia—retain a system that requires a second doctoral dissertation to be completed before a person can attain the highest academic rank, thus adding midcareer stress and maintaining an old arrangement that may have worked in the days before mass higher education but is now dysfunctional and widely criticized.

Conclusion

We are not prepared to offer our mock ranking since it would be difficult to award a top rank to a single impaired academic career system; there is much competition. In fact, global trends indicate that the path to an academic career is becoming more difficult and less attractive. This pattern will not help the improvement of universities worldwide.

For an academic system or a university to be successful, it requires an effective, fair, and transparent means of ensuring that an academic career is possible, that a professional and transparent process is attractive for scholars, and that an evaluation system is in place so that merit can be rewarded and appropriate selections made. Scholars entering the profession need access to a clear and achievable career path and assurance that high standards of performance provide career stability and success. Procedures must be rigorous and meritocratic, and institutions must have confidence that only competence will be rewarded. At the same time, evaluation systems must not be overly complicated. Mobility within academic systems is desirable. The various aspects of academic performance—including teaching, research, and service to the university and society—must be assessed, although the balance among these elements may vary according to the mission of the specific institution. Career stability and a guarantee of academic freedom must be ensured. An American-style tenure system performs this role, but there are other arrangements as well. Evaluation systems, of course, need to take into account national traditions and realities. One thing is clear—universities and systems that score high on the dysfunctionality rankings will find it difficult to succeed in a competitive world.

[*IHE* 53, Fall 2008]

17

Academic Salaries, Academic Corruption, and the Academic Career

If the academic profession does not maintain adequate income levels, academic performance throughout the system inevitably suffers. Academics must receive sufficient remuneration to live an appropriate middle-class lifestyle—not that they must be paid according to the highest international standards, local levels are generally adequate. In many, perhaps most, countries salary levels have not kept up with inflation and the academic profession has lost ground to other professional occupations. In many countries, especially in the developing world and the middle-income nations of the former Soviet Union, academic salaries are entirely inadequate to live on. In such circumstances, academic performance deteriorates, the normal life of universities becomes difficult or impossible, and the temptation of corruption lures many academics. The harsh reality is that academics must find other sources of income.

Worldwide, the design of the academic career, built up over centuries, is under threat—indeed, it is being systematically dismantled in many countries. The traditional view of academic work sees it as more than a job—instead as something of a calling. The idea that professors are devoted to "the life of the mind" is part of professional identity. These goals may seem quaint and romantic in the market-oriented 21st century, but the concept of the university as an intellectual institution and something more than a degree granting machine underlies them. If academics are allowed to pursue their traditional job of teaching and, for some but by no means all cases, research, universities can perform their traditional duties of educating the next generation of professionals, providing general learning, and creating new knowledge. For this to be sustained, however, the conditions for a "normal" academic career must survive—adequate remuneration, a realistic career path offering the likelihood of promotion and stability of employment, academic freedom to pursue teaching and research, at least a modicum of autonomy and participation in institutional governance, and the respect of society.

This does not mean that professors equal mandarins, who are free of accountability and create their own ivory tower utopias. The realities of mass higher education make this impossible. The professoriate must be differentiated by function and role, with most academics performing mainly teaching and only a minority involved in research. Accountability for academic work is necessary and appropriate. Some who work in universities are part time, and others have limited-term appointments. The argument here is that the core academic profession in every country must receive payment from the university adequate to sustain middle-class life. A substantial full-time cadre of university teachers and researchers can maintain the essential teaching, research, and governance functions of any university.

An Egyptian Example

A recent example from Egypt exemplifies the inevitable consequences of inadequate academic salaries. According to an article in the *Egyptian Gazette*, "university professors in Egypt have been accused of violating their code of ethics by greedily demanding large sums of money from their students." The article provides examples. Professors profit from selling, at high prices, their textbooks and lectures notes. These purchases are mandatory for students, since examinations are based on the books, and classes are often too crowded for students to attend. The texts are changed each year to prevent re-sale of the books. Students are also forced to pay extra to attend off-campus classes offered by professors—where the real information is provided. Sometimes theaters or even conference rooms in five-star hotels are rented to hold these off-campus tutoring sessions. One dean describes private tutoring as an "infectious disease that is gnawing away at the flesh of society." Academic staff interviewed for the article pointed out that they could not live on their academic salaries even though salaries were recently increased—an assistant professor in a public university earns around US$260 per month—hardly enough to support a family.

Other Activities

While little in-depth research has been produced on academic corruption, throughout the world newspapers and other news media are replete with examples of it. Our concern here is with professorial practices that stray from standard academic ethics. Professors in some countries routinely demand bribes to help with admissions, to raise exam grades, or to permit student cheating. Money is paid to obtain academic appointments or promotions. Decisions concerning the purchase of equipment or supplies are sometimes influenced by payoffs, and selling scientific equipment occurs. Corrupt practices of many kinds take place so that academics can supplement inadequate salaries.

Causes and Effects

It is, of course, difficult to pinpoint the causes of academic corruption. In some societies, ingrained corrupt practices at all levels influence the universities, and inadequate salaries may be just part of a larger problem. Universities cannot be insulated from societal corruption. But the root cause in many developing and middle-income countries is related to academic salaries. If that problem were solved, it would be possible to deal with professorial corruption.

In most instances, universities are not corrupt institutions. They have strong traditions of meritocracy and shared academic values. But they cannot survive systematic starvation without ethics being damaged. Providing a living wage for the academic profession, as well as maintaining the core idea of the academic career, is a necessary prerequisite for an ethical academic culture.

Adequate salaries are, however, not enough. Well-paid professors are not always productive. A culture of productive academic work necessarily includes accountability, an internal ethic of hard work, a system of evaluation that includes an objective assessment of all kinds of academic work, and a merit-based system of salary allocation and promotion. Promoting academic staff on the basis of seniority alone, the practice in many countries, works against productivity.

The case of India is illustrative. Academic salaries for full-time staff were increased several years ago to levels able to minimally support middle-class life, although at the same time, salaries for highly skilled professionals outside of the universities increased much faster. However, little was done to ensure productivity or accountability on campus. As a result, the campus culture in many universities and colleges of modest productivity, favoritism in appointments and promotions, and a lack of high academic standards remains despite salary improvements.

Conclusion

The current practice in many countries of asking academics to become entrepreneurs—by teaching in profit-making parallel programs, consulting, creating private companies, or focusing on contract research—in order to enhance their salaries may solve immediately funding shortfalls but it damages the long-term health of the university. Overreliance on part-time staffing means that there will be no one on campus who takes responsibility for the institution—there is no stability and no institutional commitment. These, and other, practices lead directly to academic corruption, not only forcing professors to enhance their incomes "by any means necessary" but also by jettisoning the traditional values and orientations of the university. The simple reality is that a healthy academic institution is an organic whole that requires adequate financial support, rigorous enforcement of traditional academic values, and at its core an academic profession committed to these values. Without this, corruption is likely to flourish and academic quality will inevitably suffer.

[*IHE* 44, Summer 2006]

18

The Overuse of Rankings

Indian Prime Minister Manmohan Singh recently chastised Indian universities for having no institutions in the "top 200" of the global higher education rankings. He sees this poor showing as an indication of the low quality of Indian higher education. Indian authorities also said that only overseas universities in the global "top 500" would be permitted to establish a branch campus or joint-degree program in India. Other countries use the global rankings for internal purposes. Singapore uses them as a benchmark and as an indicator, where scholarship students may be sent. Russia has bemoaned its poor showing, has provided extra funding for selected universities, and is considering major additional resources for a few—in order to ensure that several will be in the top ranks soon. Kazakhstan is committed to having a university in the top tier and looks to rankings as a guideline. At least one American university president has been offered a salary bonus if his university improves its rank. The list goes on.

Anatomy and Critique
There are, of course, many rankings. Most are national and some are specialized. The majority are sponsored by magazines and other for-profit organizations. Many, if not most, are worthless, because their methodologies are flawed or there is no methodology at all. Prime Minister Singh and most of the countries mentioned here refer to the three well-known international rankings. Two of these, the Academic Ranking of World Universities, popularly known as the "Shanghai rankings," and the World University Rankings of *Times Higher Education* are methodologically respectable and can be taken seriously.

But these rankings are quite limited in what they measure and thus provide only an incomplete perspective on higher education and on the universities that are ranked. The Shanghai rankings are quite clear in what is assessed—only research, research impact, and a few variables related to research—such as prizes awarded to professors and numbers of Nobel winners associated with the institution. *Times Higher Education* measures a wider array of variables. Research and its impact is at the top of the list, but reputation is also included as are several other variables—such as teaching quality and internationalization. But since there is no real way to measure teaching or internationalization, weak proxies are used. Reputation is perhaps the most controversial element in most of the national and global rankings. Even asking a selected group of academics and university leaders for their opinions about which universities are best yields questionable results. How much will physicists in Bulgaria or university rectors in Germany know about the quality of universities in India or Russia? It is not surprising, therefore, that only the Indian Institutes of Technology are ranked. They are among the few Indian institutions receiving international attention. In general, the more reputation is used as a key variable, the less accurate a ranking is likely to be. Further, respondents filling out reputational surveys for rankings will judge an institution on its research reputation—teaching excellence, national relevance, or university-university linkages are not part of the knowledge base.

In addition, certain kinds of research receive the greatest attention—the research that appears in recognized international refereed journals. The journals that are chosen for inclusion in the Web of Science, Science Citation Index, Social Science Citation Index, and a few others are considered "legitimate." This limitation dramatically privileges publication in English—the language of the vast majority of the internationally recognized journals. Further, research that adheres to the norms and values of editors and peer reviewers, who are mainly in the top Western universities, will tend to get published. The hard sciences receive much more attention than soft fields such as the arts and humanities. Universities that are strong in technology, life sciences, and related fields have significant advantages.

Distortions

Many outstanding institutions worldwide do not appear in the rankings because they do not happen to fit into the specific criteria measured. In general, specialized universities, other than those in technology, do not do well. America's elite liberal arts colleges, by most accounts offering some of the best-quality education in the world, are nowhere to be found. Universities that do not have engineering or medicine are probably undercounted. Most important, perhaps, is the disadvantages faced by developing and emerging economies. Researchers do not have easy access to the top journals, must write in English, and perhaps most important, the topics and the methodologies of the research must be appealing to editors and reviewers in the central academic powers.

The Usefulness of Rankings

To an extent, the rankings provide a way of benchmarking for the small number of research universities worldwide. By looking carefully at the structures, governance, funding, and academic cultures of the universities that do well in the rankings, lessons can be learned. Even though the budgets of the research superpowers can seldom be matched and the access of these institutions to top international talent will be impossible for most, there are global academic practices that may yield insights.

Guidelines Not Models

For India, or other developing countries, to obsess about the rankings is a mistake. There may be lessons, but not rules. It is much more important that a balanced and differentiated academic system emerges, and as part of such a system there may be a few universities that can aspire to the middle or even the upper reaches of the ranking in time. To limit academic cooperation to those universities that are listed in the global rankings is also a mistake, since many outstanding institutions do not fit the rankings model but nonetheless may be excellent global partners. When it comes to universities, one size does not fit all. The global rankings measure just one kind of academic excellence, and even here the tools of measurement are far from perfect.

[*IHE* 72, Summer 2013]

19

Rankings Season Is Here

With the arrival of the new academic year in much of the world, the rankings season must be under way. The major international rankings have appeared in recent months—the Academic Ranking of World Universities ([ARWU] the "Shanghai Rankings"), the QS World University Rankings, and the *Times Higher Education* World University Rankings (*THE*). Two important US rankings have also been published—the US *News & World Report* America's Best College Rankings and the much-delayed National Research Council's Assessment of Research Doctorate Programs. These are but a few of the rankings available on national or regional postsecondary institutions. For example, the European Union is currently sponsoring a major rankings project. In Germany, the Center for Higher Education Development has formulated an innovative approach to rankings of German universities. The list can be extended. This discussion will provide some comments on each of these rankings and on the current debate on rankings generally.

The Inevitability of Rankings

If rankings did not exist, someone would invent them. They are an inevitable result of mass higher education and of competition and commercialization in postsecondary education worldwide. Potential customers (students and their families) want to learn which of many higher education options to choose—the most relevant and most advantageous. Rankings provide some answers, to these questions. Mass higher education produced a diversified and complex academic environment, with many new academic institutions and options. It is not surprising that rankings became prominent first in the United

States, the country that experienced massification earliest as a way of choosing among the growing numbers of institutional choices. Colleges and universities themselves wanted a way to benchmark against peer institutions. Rankings provided an easy, if highly imperfect, way of doing this. The most influential, and widely criticized, general ranking is the *US News & World Report* America's Best College Ranking, now in its 17th year. Numerous other rankings exist as well, focusing on a range of variables, from the "best buys" to the best party schools and institutions that are most "wired." Most of these rankings have little validity but are nonetheless taken with some seriousness by the public.

As postsecondary education has become more internationalized, the rankings have, not surprisingly, become global as well. Almost three million students study outside their own countries; many seek the best universities available abroad and find rankings quite useful. Academe itself has become globalized, and institutions seek to benchmark themselves against their peers worldwide—and often to compete for students and staff. Academic decision makers and government officials sometimes use the global rankings to make resource choices and other decisions.

For all their problems, the rankings have become a high-stakes enterprise that have implications for academe worldwide. For this reason alone, they must be taken seriously and understood. An indication of the extent of the enterprise is the IREG Observatory on Academic Ranking and Excellence, which recently concluded its fifth conference, which attracted 160 participants from 50 countries, in Berlin.

Rankings Presume a Nonexistent Zero-Sum Game

There can only be 100 among the top-100 universities by definition. Yet, because the National University of Singapore improves does not mean, for example, that the University of Wisconsin–Madison is in decline—even if NUS rises in the rankings, perhaps forcing some other institutions down. In fact, there is room at the top for as many world-class universities that meet the accepted criteria for such institutions. Indeed, as countries accept the need to build and sustain research universities and to invest in higher education generally, it is inevitable that the number of distinguished research universities will grow. The investments made in higher education by China, South Korea, Taiwan, Hong Kong, and Singapore in the past several decades have resulted in the dramatic improvement of those countries' top universities. Japan showed similar improvements a decade or two earlier. The rise of Asian universities is only partly reflected in the rankings since it is not easy to knock the traditional leaders off their perches. The rankings undervalue the advances in Asia and perhaps other regions. As fewer American and British universities will inevitably appear in the top 100 in the future, this does not mean that their universities are in decline. Instead, improvement is taking place elsewhere. This is a cause for celebration and not hand-wringing.

Perhaps a better idea than rankings is an international categorization similar to the Carnegie Classification of Institutions of Higher Education in the United States. Between 1970 and 2005, the Carnegie Foundation provided a carefully defined set of categories of colleges and universities and then assigned placements of institutions in these categories according to clear criteria. The schools were not ranked but rather delineated according to their missions. This would avoid the zero-sum problem. Many argue that the specific ranking number of a university makes little difference. What may have validity is the range of institutions in which a university finds itself. Moreover, what may be useful is whether an institution is in a range of 15 to 25 or 150 to 170—not whether it is 17 or 154. Delineating by category might capture reality better.

Where Is Teaching in the International Rankings?

In a word—*nowhere*. One of the main functions of any university is largely ignored in all of the rankings. Why? Because the quality and impact of teaching is virtually impossible to measure and quantify. Further, measuring and comparing the quality and impact of teaching across countries and academic systems are even more difficult factors. Thus, the rankings have largely ignored teaching. The new *Times Higher Education* rankings have recognized the importance of teaching and have assigned several proxies to measure teaching. These topics include reputational questions about teaching, teacher-student ratios, numbers of PhDs awarded per staff member, and several others. The problem is that these criteria do not actually measure teaching, and none even come close to assessing quality of impact. Further, it seems unlikely that asking a cross-section of academics and administrators about teaching quality will yield much useful information. At least, *THE* has recognized the importance of the issue.

What, Then, Do the Rankings Measure?

Simply stated, rankings largely measure research productivity in various ways. This is the easiest thing to assess—indeed, perhaps the only things that can be reliably measured. The several rankings approach the topic differently. Some, especially QS, emphasize reputational surveys— what do academics around the world think of a particular university?

As a result, QS mainly assesses what a somewhat self-selected group of academics think of various universities along with some other nonreputational factors. *Times Higher Education* looks at a number of variables, including the opinions of academics; but, along with its data partner Thomson Reuters, has selected a variety of other variables—the impact of articles published as measured by citation analysis, funding for research, income from research, and several others. The Shanghai-based Academic Ranking of World Universities measures only research and is probably the most precise in measuring its particular set of variables.

Research, in its various permutations, earns the most emphasis since it is relatively easily measured but also because it tends to have the highest prestige—universities worldwide want to be research intensive and the most respected and top-ranking universities are research focused. These two factors have been a powerful force for reinforcing the supremacy of research in both the rankings and in the global hierarchy.

Centers and Peripheries

The universities and academic systems, located in the world's knowledge centers, and the scholars and scientists in these institutions not surprisingly have major advantages in the rankings. The academic systems of the major English-speaking countries such as the United States, the United Kingdom, Canada, and Australia have significant head starts. Historical tradition, language, wealth, the ability to attract top scholars and students worldwide, strong traditions of academic freedom, an academic culture based on competition and meritocracy, and other factors contribute to the dominant positions of these universities.

All of the rankings privilege certain kinds of research and thus skew the league tables. There is a bias toward the hard sciences—the STEM (science, technology, engineering, and mathematics)—which tend to produce the most articles, citations, and research funding. The rankings are biased toward universities that use English and the academics in those universities. The largest number of journals included in the relevant databases are in English, and it is easiest for native English speakers and professors at these universities to get access to the top journals and publishers and to join the informal networks that tend to dominate most scientific disciplines.

Universities in western Europe and Japan have relatively easy access to the key knowledge networks and generally adequate support. Academic institutions in Hong Kong and Singapore have the advantage of financial resources, English as the language of teaching and research, and a policy of employing research-active international staff. This trend has permitted their universities to do well in the rankings. The emerging economies, most notably China, are increasingly active as well, and they are moving from periphery to center. Even well-supported universities in peripheral regions, such as the Middle East, have disadvantages in becoming academic centers. There are strong links between the central or peripheral status of a country or academic culture and the placement of their universities in the rankings.

In the age of globalization, it is easier for academic institutions to leapfrog the disadvantages of peripherality with thoughtful planning and adequate resources. Individual academics as well as institutes and departments can also make a global mark more easily than ever before. While the barriers between centers and peripheries are more permeable, they nonetheless remain formidable.

Changing the Goalposts

Many of the rankings have been criticized for frequently changing their criteria or methodology, thus making it difficult to measure performance over time or to usefully make comparisons with other institutions. *US News & World Report* has been particularly prone to changing criteria in unpredictable ways, making it extremely difficult for the colleges and universities providing data to do so consistently. It is likely that the *Times Higher Education* rankings, in its first year, will likely change to some extent as an effort is made to improve the methodology. The Shanghai rankings have been most consistent over time, contributing no doubt to the relative stability of institutions and countries.

A 2010 Critique

It may be useful to analyze briefly the main rankings as a way of understanding their strengths and, more important, their weaknesses. While this discussion is neither complete nor based on a full analysis of the rankings, it will provide some reasons for thinking critically about them.

The QS World University Rankings are the most problematical. Between 2004 and 2009, these ranking were published with *Times Higher Education*. After that link was dropped, *Times Higher Education* is now publishing its own rankings. From the beginning, QS has relied on reputational indicators for a large part of the analysis. Most experts are highly critical of the reliability of simply asking a rather unrandom group of educators and others involved with the academic enterprise for their opinions. In addition, QS queries the views of employers, introducing even more variability and unreliability in the mix. Some argue that reputation should play no role at all in ranking, while others say it has a role but a minor one. Forty percent of the QS rankings are based on a reputational survey. This probably accounts for the significant variability in the QS rankings over the years. Whether the QS rankings should be taken seriously by the higher education community is questionable.

The Academic Ranking of World Universities (ARWU), often referred to as the Shanghai Jiao Tong rankings, are now administered by the Shanghai Rankings Consultancy. One of the oldest of the international rankings, having been started in 2003, ARWU is both consistent and transparent. It measures only research productivity, and its methodology is clearly stated and applied consistently over time. It uses six criteria, including numbers of articles published in *Science* and *Nature*, numbers of highly cited researchers as measured by Thomson Scientific, alumni and staff winning Nobel and Fields prizes, citations in Science and Social Science Citation indexes and several others. ARWU chooses 1,000 universities worldwide to analyze. It does not depend on any information submitted by the institutions themselves. Some of ARWU's criteria clearly privilege older prestigious Western universities—particularly those that have produced or can attract Nobel prizewinners. The universities tend to pay high salaries and have excellent laboratories and libraries. The various indices used also heavily rely on top-peer-reviewed journals in English, again giving an advantage to the universities that house editorial offices and key reviewers. Nonetheless, ARWU's consistency, clarity of purpose, and transparency are significant advantages.

The *Times Higher Education* World University Rankings, which appeared in September is the newest and in many ways the most ambitious effort to learn lessons for earlier rankings and provide a comprehensive and multifaceted perspective. *Times Higher Education* gets an A grade for effort, having tried to include the main university functions—research, teaching, links with industry, and internationalization. It has included reputation among the research variables and has combined that with analyses of citations, numbers of publications, degrees produced, and other measures. Disappointingly but not surprisingly, there are problems. Some commentators have raised questions about the methodologies used to count publications and citations. There are a number of inconsistencies—due to administrative problems apparently no Israeli universities are included and some of the American universities are not single campuses but rather systems are included together (examples include the University of Massachusetts, Indiana University, the University of Delaware, Kent State University, and others). This problem increases the rankings of these "systems" unfairly. If, for example, the University of California was included as a system rather than as individual campuses, it would clearly rank number one in the world. Some of the rankings are clearly inaccurate. Why do Bilkent University in Turkey and the Hong Kong Baptist University rank ahead of Michigan State University, the University of Stockholm, or Leiden University in Holland? Why is Alexandria University ranked at all in the top 200? These anomalies, and others, simply do not pass the "smell test." Let it be hoped that these, and no doubt other, problems can be worked out.

A word should be said about the long-awaited National Research Council's evaluation of American doctoral programs. This study, years late, has been widely criticized for methodological flaws as well as the fact that it is more of a historical artifact than a useful analysis of current reality. Nonetheless, the National Research Council attempted to use a much more sophisticated approach to assessment, including considering 20 key variables relating to doctoral programs. The other rankings tend to use many more arbitrary measures and weightings. Even if total success was not achieved, there are no doubt lessons to be learned.

The *US News & World Report's* annual ranking juggernaut continues. Widely criticized in the United States for the constant changes in methodology, over-reliance on reputational indicators, and oversimplifying complex reality, it is nonetheless widely used and highly influential. College and universities that score well, even if they grumble about methodological shortcomings, publicize their ranks. At least, *US News & World Report* differentiates institutions by categories—national universities, liberal arts colleges, regional institutions, and so on. This recognizes variations in mission and purpose and that not all universities are competing with Harvard and Berkeley.

Where Are We?

No doubt university rectors and presidents, government officials, and anxious students and parents from Beijing to Boston will be analyzing one or more of the rankings discussed here or the many others that exist. Decisions will be made in part based on the rankings—on funding and other support from government, on which departments and programs to build, and perhaps which programs to eliminate; and at what college or university to attend, at home or abroad, by students and their families.

In the world of rankings as in much else it is caveat emptor—the user must be fully aware of the uses and the problems, of the rankings. Too often this is not the case. The specific ranking of universities is persuasive to many users. This of course is a mistake. It is erroneous not only because of the limitation in the rankings themselves but because the rankings only measure a small slice of higher education. A government should be just as concerned about how a university fits into the higher education system as about its research-based rank. Students should be concerned about the fit between their own interests and abilities as well as the prestige of an institution. And few take into account the short-comings of the rankings themselves.

Railing against the rankings will not make them go away; competition, the need to benchmark, and indeed the inevitable logic of globalization make them a lasting part of the academic landscape of the 21st century. The challenge is to understand the nuances, uses—and misuses—of the rankings.

[*IHE* 62, Winter 2011]

20

Hong Kong's Academic Advantage*

Why is it that Hong Kong, a special administrative region of China, with a population of 7 million, has more highly ranked research universities than mainland China—with its population of 1 billion and unprecedented expenditures for establishing world-class research universities? The answers may yield important insights for the improvement of research universities everywhere.

Hong Kong's Academic Realities

Hong Kong has three universities that score well in the global rankings, and all eight of its public universities are academically respectable institutions. The three top schools—the University of Hong Kong, the Hong Kong University of Science and Technology, and the Chinese University of Hong Kong, score respectively at 34, 61, and 151 in the *Times Higher Education* 2011 rankings. The two top mainland Chinese universities, Peking University and Tsinghua University, rank at 49 and 71. The new greater China rankings, prepared by the Academic Rankings of World Universities ("Shanghai rankings"), place the three Hong Kong institutions at 3, 5, and 6; only Tsinghua University and National Taiwan University score better. The three Hong Kong institutions are medium sized by global standards—with between 10,000 and 20,000 students each. Two are comprehensive universities with medical schools, and one is a science and technology university. All were established in the 20th century—the University of Hong Kong in 1911, Chinese University of Hong Kong in 1964, and the Hong Kong University of Science

---

* With Gerard A. Postiglione

and Technology in 1991. All of Hong Kong's universities are public institutions, with good financial support from the government; and all charge students a relatively modest tuition.

The Context of Success

There are a variety of ingredients that have contributed to the success of Hong Kong's big three. It is useful to note that none of the three schools were academic powerhouses until the 1990s. The two older institutions were respectable second-tier institutions, and the Hong Kong University of Science and Technology was not established until 1991. Hong Kong decided to invest significantly in higher education in the 1990s, as the territory anticipated the transition from British colonial rule to its current status as a Special Administrative Region of China—with considerable institutional autonomy and academic freedom of action. Flush economic times permitted government investment. Hong Kong began to emphasize research universities, for several reasons. First— as one of the four tigers with Singapore, Korea, and Taiwan—Hong Kong had to keep up; and even though the government left investment in high tech to the private sector, it was willing to establish a science and technology university. Second, this was the beginning of the age of massification. As Hong Kong's postsecondary colleges and polytechnics moved toward university status, its three universities could take the step toward becoming research universities, as Hong Kong moved toward developing a diversified academic system.

Characteristics of Success

A brief overview of some of the key factors that have contributed to Hong Kong's academic success may yield some useful explanations.

"Steering" and autonomy. Hong Kong's government, through the Research Grants Council and the University Grants Committee, provides overall direction to the higher education sector; prioritized funding, combined with performance guidelines, shape university policy. At the same time, the universities have almost complete internal autonomy and self-management.

Effective governance. The University of Hong Kong stems from the British academic tradition and the Chinese University, though established by the consolidation of American missionary colleges in 1963, brought American missionary and Chinese traditions into Hong Kong's colonial framework for higher education. The Hong Kong University of Science and Technology added the American research university model and academic governance to the mix, without assaulting the status quo. All three have strong international governance arrangements that emphasize control by the academics, while at the same time strong administrative leadership. Shared governance seems to work well in Hong Kong, although all three of the universities have somewhat different approaches to it. The universities do not seem to get bogged down in endless academic bickering, nor are they ruled by autocratic administrators. There are some interesting variations between the British-influenced University of Hong Kong and the more American-oriented arrangement at the Hong Kong University of Science and Technology, though in recent years the two arrangements have begun to merge.

English dominates. English is the medium of instruction in all the universities, although both English and Chinese (the Cantonese dialect but also Mandarin) are used at the Chinese University of Hong Kong, to reflect its name. This means that Hong Kong's universities are immediately in the mainstream of global science and scholarship. Though academics at the Chinese University of Hong Kong may use Chinese as a medium of instruction, they are as capable as any to fully participate in the global scientific community through the medium of English. There is a strong orientation toward the key international academic journals; and most publications produced are in English, although in recent years Chinese publications have increased as Hong Kong academics have begun to take advantage of the impact won by publishing in the massive academic landscape on the Chinese mainland.

Internationalism. Hong Kong as a place is highly internationalized. This has always meant North America, England, and Australia but has gradually come to include more academics from the Chinese mainland and a small but increasing number of top academics, from every continent. Hong Kong is the Asian headquarters for many multinational companies, and is one of the top-three (after New York and London) international banking centers. Although its population is 95 percent Chinese, an international cosmopolitan spirit pervades. Most of the top academics at research universities have doctorates earned overseas, and many go on to academic and administrative posts in overseas universities. The universities have always seen themselves as international institutions. No other regions in Asian higher education have better access to international scholarly books and publications. There is no censorship of the Internet, and academic books that may be restricted elsewhere in Asia are all available in Hong Kong. Hong Kong's research universities hold international academic events—forums, seminars, and conferences, on a caliber of anywhere in the world.

The academic profession. Clearly the most important aspects of Hong Kong's success in higher education, academics there are relatively well treated. While they are no longer the highest-paid academics in the world, salaries compete globally, and Hong Kong is able to recruit some of the best academic minds. The universities also ensure that top scholars and scientists, including Nobel laureates, are invited to lecture; and their own academics have ample opportunities to attend international conferences. Terms and conditions of academic work—including teaching loads, administrative support, and the availability of research funding, on a competitive basis from local sources—are all globally competitive. Leaders in academic fields also play a role in external assessment of research grant applications and teaching programs. Hiring, promotion, and tenure are performance based and quite competitive, contributing to academic productivity. Hong Kong is not only able to hire talented academics globally but has a special attraction for some overseas and mainland Chinese academics, who can live in a Chinese environment, while at the same time enjoying good salaries and working conditions—superior to what is offered to most academics on the Chinese mainland. Just as important, Hong Kong offers mainland returnees an atmosphere that is not stifled by bureaucracy, where decision making is more participative and transparent and in which academic freedom and information access are unfettered. What mainly distinguishes the academic profession in Hong Kong from elsewhere is its view that personnel matters and resource allocations are largely perceived by academic staff to be made on the basis of performance measures. This was not always the case. For example, a few decades ago, the University of Hong Kong resembled a provincial British university in its academic culture. A remarkable transformation has taken place.

University leadership. The faith of the academic profession in the research universities of Hong Kong has hinged on the academic caliber of its institutional leaders. Each of the three research universities has ensured that only outstanding academics would be at the helm of their institutions. This has undoubtedly had a great deal to do with the rise of Hong Kong's universities in the international rankings. For example, the last president of the University of Hong Kong is a world-renowned geneticist, and the president of the Chinese University of Hong Kong was awarded a Nobel Prize for his work in fiber optics. The current president of the Hong Kong University of Science and Technology distinguished himself as a key assistant director of the US National Science Foundation, in charge of the Mathematical and Physical Sciences Directorate. There may be other considerations in the selection of university leaders. However, to sustain its rise in the global rankings, Hong Kong must ensure that the most significant aspects are that the most-respected global scholars and scientists are the ones that are in positions of authority at their universities.

Hong Kong and China: Useful Comparisons

The Hong Kong case has special relevance for mainland China and indicates some of the factors that may inhibit China's rise to top-academic status. While the investment in the facilities of its top research universities has been impressive in recent years, the "soft elements" of the Chinese academic system may well inhibit the system from achieving the top levels. Among these, the most prominent are governance and academic culture. China still places an inordinate emphasis on the political skill of its academic leaders—something that is understandable, given the context in which academic leaders operate on the Chinese mainland. Nevertheless, the new education blueprint for 2020 has made the "de-administration of universities" a major objective in raising the academic quality of its universities. Thus, government would take more of a steering role than a direct interventionist role in the academic life of universities, although the recent case of the South China University of Science and Technology has demonstrated the difficulty of this process. There has been a steady and unmistakable rise in the internationalism of China's research universities. The surge in the amount of Sino-foreign cooperation in higher education, including overseas campuses on Chinese soil, is an indication of progress. More presidents of top research universities have a doctorate from overseas or have spent a good deal of time there.

A key factor in the continued rise of mainland research universities relates to low academic salaries. Low-base salaries mean that academics must search for additional income through research grants, consulting, and extra teaching and, thus, pay less attention to their core academic responsibilities. A related problem is the development of a mature academic culture. Mainland China will benefit by looking at Hong Kong's recipe for academic success.

[*IHE* 66, Winter 2012]

21

The Challenges of Building a World-Class University: Lessons from Slovenia

Slovenia, a small country with a population of 2 million in the middle of central Europe, takes higher education seriously. It educates a respectable 67 percent of its age group in higher education. Its three universities enroll 81,617 students—two-thirds of them at the University of Ljubljana. Public expenditure on higher education is around 1.25 percent, not bad in the European Union context, and significantly ahead of its neighbors in the former Yugoslavia and the Balkans. Slovenian universities are arguably the best in the region. Slovenia's higher education context—and aspirations—has relevance not only for other countries with small populations but also for universities with a traditional continental European pattern of academic governance and administration.

The Context
Slovenia is committed to an egalitarian philosophy of higher education. All of the public universities have a research mission, and tuition is free for full-time undergraduate students. There is one small private university. At the end of secondary school, students who score well on the *matura* examination are, in most cases, automatically admitted to a university. Those who do not quite meet the standards can often enroll in an evening or other part-time programs, where tuition is charged, and end up with the same degree as the regular students. The pattern of "dual track" study with variations in tuition and admissions standards—now common in some European countries, China, and elsewhere—distorts

student admissions, teaching loads for professors, and creates other problems. Tuition is also charged for doctoral study.

In common with many universities in continental Europe, rectors are elected by the academic staff, with additional participation of students (who control 20% of the votes). They serve four-year terms and can be reelected. Similarly, deans are also elected, and a strong ethos of autonomy exists throughout the academic system. Campus interest groups—including autonomous and well-funded student unions and professor interest groups—are powerful.

A 2011 National Higher Program for Slovenia, recently approved by Parliament, lists a range of initiatives for reforms in higher education and research, by 2020. These factors are aimed at improving Slovenia's research infrastructure and output, as well as boosting the country's internationalization and to some extent diversifying the higher education system; although the list of innovations is long and the guidelines for specific implementation is limited. The devil is, of course, in the details, and implementing significant change in Slovenia's consensus-driven system will probably be a challenge, particularly since higher education attracts a good deal of public interest.

World-Class for Slovenia?

What might a world-class university look like in the Slovenian context? Certainly, no Slovenian university can aim to compete with Berkeley or Oxford. The country could not finance a Berkeley nor does it have the population base to support an Oxford. But at least one Slovenian institution, no doubt the University of Ljubljana, could become a globally competitive university in a number of academic fields and internationally visible as an institution. As a nation that depends on its human resources that sits in a strategic place in Europe, the 2011 National Higher Education Program makes sense, although it does not seem to go far enough in concentrating financial and human resources.

The strategy makes a sharp break with past thinking. At least it recognizes the need for Slovenia to work harder on higher education. The traditional view seemed to be general satisfaction with an academic environment that is good but not great. Assuming that Slovenia at some point will wish to play in the academic big leagues, what would be required to fulfill existing possibilities and secure a place in the European and global knowledge economy?

The Prospects

Paths to academic excellence vary according to national and institutional circumstances, but it is easy to identify some of the Slovenian realities that create problems for improvement—challenges that are shared by many countries and institutions. While the possibilities for significant improvement may objectively be present, policy and governance issues pose daunting obstacles. The following factors will, at least in part, determine Slovenia's academic future.

Governance. In common with many European universities, top academic leaders in Slovenia are elected to four-year terms of office. They typically return to the faculty, following administrative service. Rectors, for example, are elected by the academic community—including academic staff and students, who have 20 percent of the votes. Rectors and deans, typically, govern by consensus and are seldom willing to exercise leadership that may create strong opposition in the academic community. This means that universities seldom, if ever, have strong internal leadership with the option to make decisions that may create dissent or controversy. Elected top management will be unable to implement the serious decisions that are inevitably required for building academic excellence.

Funding. Full-time undergraduate students pay no tuition in Slovenia—although fees are charged for part-time study and some graduate programs. Thus, universities are largely dependent on direct government funding. In mass higher education systems, public funding can never provide both access and excellence; the costs are simply too high. For Slovenia to achieve world-class excellence, it will need to find additional funds to support an expensive research university; and it is unrealistic to expect total state funding. There is probably no alternative to charging tuition to all students—of course, with appropriate scholarship assistance for students who may not be able to afford the costs. At the same time, the state will need to enhance funding and to ensure that required resources are available over the long term. Additional income can be obtained by enhanced cooperation with industry and other agencies. Excellent universities can prosper only with sustained funding.

Academic differentiation. Slovenia's three public universities are all research universities and are similarly funded. Even in a small country, it is necessary to differentiate academic missions among the universities. Slovenia can afford one research-intensive university, the University of Ljubljana. The other institutions, which are newer and much smaller, must focus on teaching at the undergraduate level. Financial and human resources must be carefully concentrated. It will, of course, be quite controversial to strip or severely constrain existing universities from some of their current roles and to ensure that research and doctoral education is carefully limited in the future.

"Steering." Determining broad academic directions and policies cannot be left to the academic community alone. Broad "steering" of higher education policy for the nation can only be developed and implemented by the government. While consultation with stakeholders, especially the academics themselves, is necessary, difficult decisions will inevitably be made by outsiders. Further, continuing governmental supervision of university policy is required to keep the system "on track." This may be particularly difficult in Slovenia's consensus-driven society, where higher education is frequently a political concern.

Selective excellence. Few universities can afford to be world class in all specialties. For a small country, careful selections will be required as to what fields and disciplines can be truly world class and which should be "merely excellent." Based on national needs, economic realities, and current academic strengths and interests, a limited number of areas—including interdisciplinary and cutting-edge fields—can be selected for concentration. Targeted funds and other resources can be provided.

Internationalization. A fine line always stands between serving national obligations and playing in the international big leagues. If the University of Ljubljana desires to achieve a world-class status, it must focus on further internationalization. This includes offering more academic programs in English; enhancing its exchange relationships; looking first to provide strong leadership to central and eastern Europe and the former Soviet Union; and, to some extent, engaging with North America and emerging Asia. Slovenia is an excellent site for research on central European themes, and the university can build its interdisciplinary strengths in understanding the challenges and possibilities of the former Yugoslavia and the region.

However, the balance between national needs and concerns and internationalization is not easy to achieve. Particularly for a small country, the universities are at the center of intellectual life and central institutions for maintaining and enhancing national language and culture. At the same time, the universities are among the most internationalized institutions in the country, and the pressures are great to increasingly engage with the rest of the world. In the Slovenian case, these forces are particularly complex, since they involve the Bologna agenda, working with the Balkans, and to some extent a broader international agenda.

The Future

Slovenia, a small country with a favorable geographical position in the middle of Europe and with a good academic infrastructure, has the potential for excellence. It already includes perhaps the best university in the region. Reaching for world-class excellence is a challenge, but this standard is not impossible. For a country dependent on its human resources, university development is a logical step. If Singapore can become a knowledge hub, why not Slovenia?

[*IHE* 68, Summer 2012]

22

Is There a Future for Branch Campuses?

Branch campuses seem to be the flavor of the month or, perhaps, the decade. Universities, mostly but not exclusively from the developed and mainly English-speaking countries, have established overseas branches worldwide—mainly in developing and emerging economies. The Observatory on Borderless Higher Education counted 162 branch campuses in 2009, with American universities accounting for 48 percent of the total. No doubt, the number of branches has increased significantly since then. The Arabian Gulf has received a great deal of global attention since several countries have welcomed—and paid for—branch campuses, as part of their higher education growth strategies. For example, Education City in Doha, Qatar, currently hosts six American universities and one from Britain. Bahrain, the United Arab Emirates, and other Gulf countries have additional branch campuses of foreign universities. Singapore predates the Gulf as a higher education hub.

Given this boom in branches, several fundamental questions need to be raised: what are branch campuses? Are they sustainable over time? What unique service do they render to students and the academic community?

What Is a Branch?
There is no generally accepted definition. Most observers seem to agree that an "international branch campus" is an entity pertaining to a university whose primary location is in one country, which operates in another and offers its own degree in that country. Upon successful

completion of the course program, fully undertaken at the unit abroad, students are awarded a degree from the foreign institution. This definition excludes joint-degree programs, twinning arrangements, overseas campuses serving students from the home university, degree franchising, and other international ventures. In a few cases, branch campuses offer the opportunity for students at the branch to study at the home university for part of their program, and some offer "study abroad" facilities for students from the home campus.

This simple definition must be considered in a fundamental way. Are the students at the overseas campus receiving essentially the same educational experience as they would experience on the home campus? Is the quality of instruction equivalent? Are the professors from the home campus? Are the facilities broadly equivalent—taking into account that it would be impossible to duplicate New York's Washington Square campus in Abu Dhabi? In other words, is a student experiencing the same, or close to the same, education as at the home campus? It is not enough to put a university's name on the degree. The actual quality and at least a semblance of the academic experience and culture at the home campus must be provided for a branch campus to deserve to offer a university's degree. Anything less "dilutes the brand" and should not be called a branch.

Questions of Sustainability
With a few exceptions, branch campuses have been established fairly recently, so that there are few clear lessons to be drawn yet from limited experience. Still, a number of questions concerning sustainability must be asked.

Enrollments. Will branch campuses be able to enroll students of the same quality as their home-campus students over time? A number of problems in this respect are already evident. The University of New South Wales, for example, closed its branch campus in Singapore in 2007, after less than a year—due to low enrollments. Most of the American branches in the Gulf are reportedly under enrolled. In that region, particularly, it is unclear whether there are a sufficient number of young people with the requisite interests and academic accomplishments to fill the existing branch campuses, not to mention new ones.

Some of the branches see possibilities for enrollment from the Indian subcontinent, with its large population of underserved students. Yet, a recent survey showed that prospective Indian students prefer to study in the United States rather than at an American branch campus in the Gulf or, for that matter, in India itself. They would like the full experience of American culture and, perhaps, the possibility of staying in the United States to work following graduation. However, studying at a branch campus provides neither of these opportunities. Data from China indicate that students are not willing to pay US-level tuition at branch campuses of American universities in China, and they worry about the quality of faculty and programs.

Branch campuses in the Gulf are counting on significant numbers of female students from the region, assuming that many families will not want to have their daughters studying in the West but would prefer a regional institution—although 21 percent of Saudi Arabian students abroad, largely in Western countries, are women. Clearly, the assumptions are faulty. Furthermore, the small population base in the Gulf means that the numbers of students with high-academic qualifications are limited. To make matters even more complicated, both the branch campuses and local universities often need to provide up to a year of preparatory study for many students before full admission is possible—due to a combination of inadequate English-language skills and inadequate secondary school preparation. For selective universities, like Carnegie Mellon or New York University, it is highly questionable whether the pool of qualified candidates will be large enough to become sustainable over time.

While hard data are impossible to obtain, some reports have revealed that most branch campuses have not as yet met enrollment targets. Enrollments are hard to predict and depend on many variables, including changing political and social circumstances. It is not clear how the current unrest in the Middle East will impact the branch campuses in the region. As more branch campuses are established in educational hubs worldwide, there will be increased competition among them.

Faculty and staff. A branch campus requires home campus faculty to provide a real academic experience of the sponsoring university. This does not mean a few faculty members just fly in for "intensive" weekend courses. Will branch campuses be able to lure faculty members, for a semester or longer, from the home to an overseas campus? Residential faculty are necessary. Moreover, temporary adjunct faculty located in the region or local residents with doctorates awarded by the main campus of the university will not suffice. Home campus faculty must be willing to teach at the branch for a year or more. Again, the idea of a branch campus is to replicate the academic and other experience of the home university. Similarly, key administrators and support staff in student affairs and other areas must belong to the home campus to provide the spirit of the home university or at least have experience at the home campus.

Experience shows that it is quite difficult to convince home campus faculty to teach in an overseas branch campus for extended periods of time, even when salary and other benefits are attractive. Yet, even once the small group of internationally minded faculty and staff have volunteered to go abroad, convincing others to go is all but impossible. Uprooting working spouses and children is not easy. Research-active faculty—especially in the hard sciences, where laboratories at the branch cannot match those at home—will also be reluctant to leave their labs.

Funding. Branch campuses of prestigious universities receive generous start-up funding from host countries, institutions, property developers, or other entities. Typically, little up-front investment is provided by the home university and in some cases, such as the Gulf, hefty subsidies. However, significant nonmonetary expenses include the time spent by a myriad of administrators and faculty for planning, negotiations with host governments and institutions, and other aspects. Developing curricula, implementing personnel policies, and working with a variety of stakeholders all involve time—and, indirectly, money.

Sustained funding as the branch campus develops is another challenge. Most universities do not want the branch to be a drain on home campus resources, and indeed some institutions expect overseas ventures to earn a profit. For public universities, legal requirements on public funds are an added challenge, given restrictions on spending public funds overseas. Branch campuses may be under considerable pressure to "break even" quickly. Where there are sponsors with deep pockets, as in the Gulf, pressures will be less intense, but the branch campuses will eventually need to be financially sustainable.

While there are little if any data available, it seems that the most financially successful branch campuses are those sponsored by less-prestigious universities and other educational providers, which offer programs that are inexpensive to provide and have a ready interest abroad. Quality standards are often low, and careful attention is given to the "bottom line," with little regard for local relevance.

A quality-branch campus, even if it is small and specialized, requires careful financial planning in a context, which includes many variables that are difficult to measure or predict. The cost of coordination and administration at the home campus, direct instruction, maintaining appropriate enrollment and income levels, and other variables are extraordinarily difficult to forecast.

Academic Freedom
Worries have been raised about academic freedom at branch campuses. Although key leaders and relevant agreements guarantee academic

freedom, many faculty are worried. What happens, some say, if a faculty member at a Dubai branch invites an Israeli speaker, or one in China invites the Dalai Lama or writes an op-ed highly critical of the authorities. How will authorities in countries without a stellar academic freedom record handle the branch campuses?

Home Campus Politics

Branch campus initiatives are typically proposed by top university management and not by the faculty or students. They may be seen as a way of boosting the university's global image, contributing to internationalization, earning income, or a way to address other institutional strategic goals. The larger academic community is seldom involved in either planning or executing the branch campus initiative. Indeed, it is often hard to convince the faculty and students that branch campuses are worth the additional work, risk, and commitments required. Without faculty "buy in," success is difficult. Reports of significant campus grumbling at New York University have been published, and campus opposition was cited as one of the reasons for the failure of Michigan State University's branch campus in the Gulf. Most recently, criticism at Yale University concerning that university's partnership with the National University of Singapore, due to concerns about academic freedom and other issues has emerged in the media. International ventures have frequently been subject to considerable complaints in Australian universities as well, with members of the academic community criticizing commercial motivations and opposing straying from the university's core academic mission. Press reports concerning virtually all branch campus initiatives have featured disputes between administrators and segments of the faculty.

Overseas Uncertainties and Changing Policies

The 21st century is the age of globalization. It is also an era of political instability and the transformation of national policies and priorities in many parts of the world. Branch campuses operate in a national context. The current Arab Spring political and social unrest is an example of how drastically and unpredictably political circumstances change. It is impossible to know how the political and social transitions in the Middle East will affect branch campuses in the medium and long run.

The current debate in India—one of the world's largest potential student markets—about government policies relating to branch campuses and other foreign higher education initiatives—is yet another example of how unpredictable this environment can be. The terms and conditions of international involvement will be dramatically altered;

and the practical aspects of how these policies will be implemented, in a country famous for opaque regulations, will only emerge over time. Branch campuses are vulnerable to changing and sometimes unstable environments.

Differing Expectations

Experience shows that at times conflicting expectations of the sponsoring university and the host country or sponsor can result in serious problems. Contractual agreements may be interpreted alternatively—sometimes leading to conflicts among participating parties or even the closure of the branch. A number of these conflicts resulting from differing or interpretations of agreements are, even in this early stage of the branch campus phenomenon, already evident. The problems may be exacerbated when one side—usually the host country—is investing the bulk of the funds.

A Bubble?

Obviously, numerous and fundamental problems are facing branch campuses. Even if the basic concept is viable, the risks are substantial. If one accepts the enthusiastic comments and the range of plans and start-ups, there may be a bubble in the making. A necessary episode to recall is that 20 or more American universities rushed to Japan in the 1980s to start branches, but only 2 survived. Exactly the same kinds of misunderstandings, insufficient advance planning, unrealistic expectations on both sides, and cross-national confusion that can be seen today led to the failure of most of the Japanese ventures. The lesson—caveat everyone!

[*IHE* 65, Fall 2011]

23

Twinning and Branch Campuses: The Professorial Obstacle

Branch campuses, twinning arrangements, and other manifestations of cross-border higher education are booming. Universities in Europe, Australasia, and North America see a huge market by offering their degrees in other countries. At the same time, Singapore and several of the states in the Arabian Gulf have identified themselves as educational centers and are attracting international higher education providers. In the Gulf, there is even competition for attracting overseas universities. China has opened its doors to foreign institutions, and India is moving in this direction.

While there are no accurate numbers, more than 500 branch campuses exist worldwide—plus thousands of "twinned" programs. In addition, the phenomenon of the "American University of . . ." manifests another trend in cross-border higher education. There are a dozen or more of such universities, some of which have a direct link with a US university while many simply use the name "American" and offer a US-style curriculum in English in a non-US setting. If the General Agreement on Trade in Services (GATS) becomes part of the structure of international academic arrangements, the numbers of all kinds of cross-border institutions will increase even faster.

One significant problem exists with these arrangements. Who is teaching the students at these branch campuses? What does a degree from a university signify if the teaching staff are not from the university offering the degree? To use the McDonald's analogy—is the meal (degree) a true McDonald's hamburger if only the recipe (the curriculum) comes from McDonalds. The rest of the process—the ingredients (facilities) and the cooks (professors)—are local, rather than from the sponsoring institution. Should a university in the United Kingdom (or another country) claim to offer a degree overseas if only the curriculum is from the sponsoring school, perhaps along with an element of quality control?

With little data indicating the proportion of faculty members from the home universities teaching at branch or twinning campuses, anecdotal evidence shows that the numbers are small and most of the teaching is carried out by professors who are not faculty from the sponsoring institution. Even when they do come from the home university, faculty teaching at branch or twinned campuses are generally not the "star" research-active professors.

It is not known if some of the recent high-prestige universities that have entered the branch campus business—the University of Chicago, the Cornell University Medical School, the University of Nottingham, and others—have a different profile than the many more average institutions thus far engaged.

The Background of Teachers
Many faculty members are hired locally—some "moonlighting" from a local university. Other "local hires" are full-time staff, obtained from the local academic market or attracted away from local or regional institutions. Some faculty are natives of the country of the sponsoring university but not faculty members at that institution. For example, an American university in Singapore might hire an American working in Japan or Taiwan. PhD holders who are teaching part time or on short-term assignments in the home country may also be attracted to work overseas. The sponsoring university generally tries to ensure that these faculty have a doctoral degree from a respectable institution—insofar as possible from the country where the sponsoring university is located.

Attracting Top-Quality Faculty
At branch campuses this task may not be easy, particularly on an assignment of a year or more. Except for a few specialists in the culture where the branch is located or professors committed to learning about foreign cultures, an overseas assignment as a full-time member of the academic staff at a university in Europe, North America, or Australia may not lure prominent faculty. In addition to the challenges of uprooting families, finding schools for children, and the like, an overseas assignment disrupts the rhythm of academic life. For younger professors seeking to obtain tenure and promotion, an overseas assignment is

particularly dangerous. It will inevitably disrupt a research agenda and in the sciences may make research impossible given the lack of equivalent laboratory equipment and staff. Since branch campuses are always oriented toward teaching rather than research, teaching loads are often higher than at the home university. Libraries and other facilities are never the same either.

Many branch campuses offer faculty members from the home university additional perquisites—such as housing, transportation for families, payment of school fees, and others. In some cases, salary supplements are provided, and there is usually a tax advantage. But even these benefits may not produce a sufficient attraction.

As a result of these factors, the professors teaching at branch campuses are seldom full-time research-active faculty from the home university. If from the home institution, they are often senior staff close to retirement or those with fewer commitments at home. Most are not from the home university. Relevant academic departments at home often must approve the academic qualifications of these professors and offer them some kind of temporary appointment to legitimize their appointments.

Conclusion

Does an academic degree mean that a student has studied at the university offering the degree? Does it mean that he or she has been taught by the faculty of that institution? Does it mean that the curriculum and language of instruction of the home university have been used? Is it enough that the home institution has approved the qualifications of the teaching staff and that the general conditions of teaching are considered to be satisfactory? Should teaching be provided by faculty members who are actually on the home institution's staff, or is it acceptable that an itinerant but qualified collection of teachers do the work? Is it acceptable that the prestigious universities whose fame in their home countries is based on excellence in research as well as teaching provide an academic environment in the branch campus almost exclusively devoid of research? Cross-border academic cooperation and transnational higher education are characteristics of the 21st century, but it is necessary to carefully examine the realities in order to assess quality and effectiveness.

[*IHE* 48, Summer 2007]

24

Franchising—The McDonaldization of Higher Education

Almost 20 percent of students studying for a British first academic degree are not residing in the United Kingdom but rather pursuing their degree at one of Britain's 13 branch campuses or, much more likely, at a foreign institution that has franchised a British degree. More than 400 franchise arrangements were reported in 2008. The UK institution provides the curriculum, learning materials, quality assurance and, most important, the right to award a British degree. Universities in other countries are also involved in franchising; Australia and the United States are examples. There are even multinational franchising and twinning operations; for example, a British university and an Indian institute offer degrees in Oman.

At a branch, the home institution is, at least to some extent, "on the ground" overseas and guides hands-on direction for teaching and local supervision. Franchising is the provision of the curriculum and a degree without direct involvement. Franchising is exactly what McDonald's does. The McDonald's corporation sells the right to "brand" its products so long as the franchisee adheres to strict standards and policies. Thus, a Big Mac tastes the same in Chicago or Shanghai. "Inputs" (potatoes, meat, the "special sauce") are carefully monitored. Business practices are stipulated, and the "brand image" closely monitored and protected. There is modest latitude for local adaptation. For example, a Big Mac in Riyadh is halal, and one can find a McPork in Bucharest. The purpose of the entire enterprise is to earn profits for the franchisee and for the corporation.

One difference between McDonalds and a higher education franchise is that a McDonald's franchise requires a significant investment by the franchisee—in facilities, equipment, and the like. In many cases, an education franchise just needs to rent space with little additional investment from either side. More worrisome, an easy exit is possible for either party with the possibility of leaving students in the lurch.

Franchising is yet another example of the commodification of higher education, and the entire purpose of the operation is to make money.

What's Wrong with It?

If one accepts that nonprofit higher education institutions at home should operate as profit-making businesses overseas, nothing is fundamentally wrong. But a number of questions must be raised. Concerns have been expressed by quality-assurance agencies and in the British media that several universities—generally those at the lower end of the pecking order—have been caught offering substandard products overseas or at least not adequately monitoring the degree programs offered in their names, thus sullying the reputation of British higher education. It is very hard to adequately monitor what is being done in the name of an institution far away.

In a recent article in the *Guardian*, a senior administrator at the University of Nottingham, which has several branch campuses in Asia, notes that—in franchise or twinning arrangements—the overseas partner may have the UK curriculum; but it may not be taught with the same ethos that characterizes the home campus. An emphasis on interactive learning or critical thinking, for example, may be missing. In other words, the form but not necessarily the substance of education may be provided by the franchisee. Adequate quality assurance is not easy. Home evaluators may not be aware of conditions overseas; and in any case, the logistics are difficult and often expensive.

All of this also begs the question as to whether the curriculum offered for most specializations in the United Kingdom or in other developed countries will be appropriate for the needs of developing or middle-income countries. Yet, the essence of the franchise arrangement is that the "product" offered should be the same as at the home institution.

While no one has researched who are the franchise providers in developing and middle-income countries, they seem to be a variety of agencies. Some are private universities and other educational institutions. Some are property developers or other business interests, wishing to enter the lucrative higher education market or add an education facility to a new shopping mall or condominium complex. There may well be nothing wrong with these sponsors, but it balances the educational mission against other business interests.

Higher education franchising seems to be a growing phenomenon. As with all commercial investment in higher education, there are significant possibilities for problems. So far, the franchisers seem to be working on the McDonalds principle. It would be interesting to ask why no one is looking at the educational equivalent of Intercontinental Hotels—aiming at a higher-end market segment-—as a better model.

[*IHE* 66, Winter 2012]

25

The Costs and Benefits of "Open Access"

The Harvard Faculty of Arts and Sciences recently joined the "open access" movement, urging its professors to post their research on an open access Harvard Web site (while adding an "opt out" choice for professors who wish to submit their work to traditional journals). In this way, Harvard professors have joined a growing chorus of critics of the traditional journal publishing system by offering its research and analysis without cost to all readers through the Internet. The basic argument claims that knowledge should be free to everyone and that the Internet permits easy worldwide access. This philosophical commitment is linked to revulsion against the increasingly monopolistic and predatory practices of the multi-national journal publishers.

For Harvard, the decision is relatively cost free. Its institutional prestige and the prominence of many of its faculty will ensure that scholars gravitate to its Web site and that the work of its researchers will not be ignored. Similarly, the Massachusetts Institute of Technology initiated its open courseware program, which brought most of MIT's courses to the Internet to be accessed by all, being praised as a major contribution to knowledge—as indeed it is.

But a significant downside exists. This movement may well ensure that scholars prominent in the world of knowledge remain a dominant force, while recognition of the work of others may prove to be more difficult. Open access after all does ensure that knowledge will be equally used. This practice simply places material on the Internet to join the exponentially expanding universe of information. The problem, of course, is one of selection. How does a user of research select the best and most relevant material from the vast array of information currently available?

The Traditional System

The traditional scholarly journal provides a means of selection. The peer-review system, however imperfect it is, does a reasonably good job of vetting research and scholarship and publishing what is considered by thoughtful experts to be the most effective approach. Journal editors to some extent control the flow of manuscripts, and recognized experts anonymously evaluate them. The most deserving articles are then published. The journals themselves are ranked, customarily by the informal subcultures of the disciplines and, more recently, by the much criticized "impact factors" and other bibliometric measures.

New journals, generally part of the traditional system, were established to reflect new scientific and scholarly research, academic and societal needs, and interdisciplinary trends that have enlivened scholarship in recent decades. Some of these journals have gained prominence, while others have not. The key contribution of this system is that it provides a reasonably effective means of peer review and selection. Users are given an easy—sometimes too easy—way of selecting what is worthwhile knowledge and deciding what might best be ignored.

An Out-Of-Control System

Unfortunately, the traditional journal system has come under a multifaceted attack in recent years. The most important reality is that the system has become commercialized. Major multinational publishers, such as Springer and Elsevier, have purchased many existing journals and have dramatically increased subscription prices. Most affected are journals in the biomedical and natural sciences but in other fields as well. This trend has led to dramatic price increases that have caused problems for academic libraries, the traditional purchasers of journals. These publishers and many other smaller, for-profit, firms have created new journals, in part to serve the needs of an expanding knowledge base but also simply to create more profit-making titles. In addition, the big producers are increasingly "bundling" their journals and insisting that libraries purchase large numbers of them through electronic networks— the more journals, the higher the price. A contributing factor includes the growing competitiveness of academe itself and the need of academics to publish more to obtain promotion and salary increases.

The academic accountability movement has strengthened the traditional journal system, through the positive impact of the increasingly important citation analyses and impact factors. While these measures are far from perfect and tend to disadvantage scholarship from developing countries and other peripheral systems, they are widely used to determine academic promotions, university and departmental rankings, and for other purposes in a competitive academic system. Research assessment exercises, such as the one in England, count heavily on impact factors. Universities in China, Norway, and Israel, among many others, pay their professors to publish in internationally recognized journals. It is worth noting that the citation analyses are now in the hands of for-profit companies.

The corporatization and overexpansion of journals have created the environment for the open access movement. Academics, librarians, and some administrators think they have found a way around the increasingly expensive and monopolistic journal system—bypassing them altogether.

Problems

There are several problems with open access. Essentially, peer review is eliminated and all knowledge becomes equal. The current outlook implies "let the buyer beware," but most customers lack the expertise to make good choices. There is no quality control on the Internet, from a Wikipedia article to an essay by a distinguished researcher. In a strange way, open access may benefit those already at the top of the knowledge system. A Harvard open access Web site is likely to attract readers simply because of its world-class name. A less well-known institution in a developing country, for example, would likely gain less attention, not to mention a posting by a little-known scholar at a peripheral institution. While the traditional journals also tend to privilege scholars working at top institutions, at least the peer-review system gave some chance for publication in recognized journals. Essentially, open access means there is no objective way of measuring the quality of research without each individual evaluating it. If the traditional journals and their peer-review systems are no longer operating, there is anarchy in the evaluation of scholarship. Counting the number of times an article is accessed is possible, but it is quite likely that the randomness of a Google search will skew such evaluations. Researchers will have no accurate way of assessing quality in scholarly publication.

A Way Forward?

The old practice may well be the best, although flawed, way of communicating research. Scholarly journals owned by academic societies or universities or other nonprofit publishers provide a filter and peer review. The more innovative nonprofit publishers, such as the Johns

Hopkins University Press and its Project MUSE, creatively used the Internet for distribution. Prices were not exorbitant. The recent decision by the American Anthropological Association to lease their journals to a for-profit publisher, which has already raised prices, seems like a move in a negative direction. Without question, the proliferation of knowledge and the increasing complexity of dissemination through the Internet has creased unprecedented strains on the knowledge communication system. Open access, while it seems like an easy panacea, has problems that deserve careful consideration.

[*IHE* 52, Summer 2008]

26

Anarchy, Commercialism, and "Publish or Perish"*

In recent years, scholars worldwide have found themselves under increasing pressure to publish more, especially in English-language "internationally circulated" journals that are included in globally respected indices such as the ISI Citations. As a result, journals in these networks have been inundated by submissions and many of them accept as few as 10 percent of papers, and in some cases fewer. Given that too few journals or other channels exist to accommodate all the articles written, there has been a proliferation of new publishers offering additional journals in every imaginable field. Complementing the growing demand for new outlets of scholarly work, clever people have understood that new technology has created confusion as well as opportunities and that money can be made in the knowledge communication business.

Fake and Low-Quality Journals

Not surprisingly, a large number of "bottom feeders" are now starting "journals" with the sole goal of earning a quick profit and enriching their owners. One of these new journals charges prospective authors a "transaction fee" of US$500, to be published. Others have alternative ways of exploiting unsophisticated authors. These so-called journals have impressive sounding names and lists of prominent advisory editors—some who have in fact never been asked to serve. Peer reviewing is touted, but

---

* With Brendan Rapple

one suspects that anyone who pays the fee can get published. Clearly, authors are not served by journals without academic standing and which will not be read nor cited by anyone. Many of these sham journals are in the sciences, with computer science being well represented. The primary problem, of course, is that it is increasingly difficult for potential users to discern respectable journals from the new fakes. A quite useful resource is Jeffrey Beall's *List of Predatory, Open-Access Publishers* (http://carbon. ucdenver.edu/~jbeall/Beall%27s%20List%20of%20Predatory,%20 Open-Access%20Publishers%202012.pdf). Other options include what may be called pseudo scholarly journals. A prime example is the *Australasian Journal of Bone and Joint Medicine* published by Elsevier, a major multinational publisher. According to the *Scientist* (http://classic.the-scientist.com/blog/display/55750/), from 2002–2005 Elsevier was paid by the pharmaceutical company Merck—to publish articles in that journal that were favorable to Merck's drugs Vioxx and Fosamax. Merck's financial involvement in the journal was not disclosed. Elsevier later admitted that it had employed a similar disregard of normal peer-review practice in eight other of its journals, in the early 2000s.

As well as exploitative journals with a primary goal to make money rather than to advance scholarship, a profusion exists of "legitimate" journals, mediocre at best—publishing articles that really should not be published. The major multinational publishers of these journals have assembled large "stables" of them packaged and sold at high prices to libraries. Though many of these periodicals are supposedly peer-reviewed, the standard is frequently low, and much weak research is accepted for publication. Many faculty probably rationalize that being published somewhere is better than not being published at all. A 21st century paradox is that while it is ever more difficult to get published in a top-tier journal, it is now easier than ever to get published.

The Publish or Perish Syndrome

Surely, the still vibrant "publish or perish" syndrome must bear some of the blame. Universities increasingly demand more publications for promotion, salary increases, or even job security. Further, the pressure has increased to publish in English-language journals, even for scholars in non-English medium academic environments. Far too many academic institutions—a large majority of ones that mainly focus on teaching—insist that their faculty publish. This, their administrators believe, will improve their rankings. Of course, publishers step in to create new journals, which publish these frequently mediocre research articles. Moreover, instead of publishing all their research results in one article, too many authors stretch them out to multiple articles or write repetitively just to increase their publications. Thus, pressure is created on scholars in many fields, who must consult an exponentially increasing number of articles—many of which are worthless. Administrators are happy that their faculty publish; the publishers are delighted to sell more subscriptions; and the game goes on.

Exploding Costs of Journals and Knowledge Products

An excessive number of journals are exorbitantly priced. *Ulrichsweb Global Serials Directory* lists over 141,000 academic and scholarly journals, of which 64,000 are peer-reviewed. Clearly, libraries cannot afford to keep up with such numbers; for a long time, libraries have been canceling journals, due to the ever-escalating cost of serials. For years, the cost of journals has been increasing at a far higher rate than the Consumer Price Index, at a time when library budgets have generally been decreasing. The highest journal costs are invariably in the sciences (the average price of chemistry journals in 2011 was $4,044, that of physics ones was $3,499). The cost of some journals are indeed astronomical, for example $24,048 annually for *Brain Research*, $20,269 for *Tetrahedron*, and $17,258 for *Chemical Physics Letters*—all three journals published by Elsevier. John Wiley is another publisher whose journals are frequently extremely expensive. An institutional subscription to Wiley's Journal of Comparative Neurology will be $30,860, in 2012. Though journals in non-hard-science disciplines tend to be substantially cheaper, they are also often subject to high-cost increases. *Library Journal's* 2011 Periodicals Price Survey reveals that journals in language and literature had a 29 percent cost increase from 2009 to 2011. Philosophy and religion were next with a 22 percent increase, followed by agriculture, anthropology, and arts and architecture being tied for third at 17 percent.

Another problem for libraries is the bundling in subscription packages of hundreds of journals that often range widely in quality. With the bundling model, the library cannot select specific journals and refuse others. Libraries are locked into a deal that often results in the acquisition of poor-quality journals with few readers. Bundling is a practice for publishers to sell journals that few libraries would subscribe to if they were to be selected individually. An additional difficulty is the nondisclosure agreements that some publishers require libraries to sign. These agreements forbid libraries from disclosing the cost and terms of journal package subscriptions.

Potential Solutions

Is there any solution to this periodicals' crisis? Several strategies spring to mind. Scholars can refuse to serve on editorial boards, submit articles, or act as peer reviewer for journals that are manifestly of poor quality and/or are excessively priced. Those applying for promotion and funding can be limited to submitting, say, five or six seminal publications—the point being that the quality of one's research should count for more than quantity.

Open-access e-journals hold strong promise. Many scholarly organizations and universities have created new open-access journals that are reliably peer-reviewed and are backed by respected scholars. There are over 7,000 free, quality-controlled scholarly journals in the *Directory of Open Access Journals* (doaj.org). Some of these publications have achieved a high level of respectability and acceptance, while, admittedly, others are struggling, and there are no doubt some that are of poor quality and little relevance. It is early in the open-access movement. If successful, this movement can be an important vehicle for eradicating economic barriers to accessing scholarship. Moreover, if universities and scholarly societies, through expanding open access, can wrest more control of both the production and diffusion of scholarship away from commercial publishers, legitimate and illegitimate, as well as quality control and prices could be placed on a surer footing.

It is undeniable that presently technology and globalization have brought anarchy to the communication of knowledge in academe and have created serious problems for the academic profession, in a time of increased competition. A meaningful solution will take much dialogue and probably significant changes to how scholarship is diffused, as well as, rewarded.

[*IHE* 67, Spring 2012]

27

The Ambiguities of Working with Third-Party Recruiters[*]

International student mobility is big business. Approximately, 2.8 million students study abroad, distributing at least US$50 billion around the globe annually. Most international students come from developing or middle-income countries, the majority from East and South Asia, and most are self-financed. They contribute major revenues to the institutions and countries where they study and of course represent a key part of the internationalization of universities.

The number of students pursuing opportunities abroad is expanding and no longer limited to individuals from elite backgrounds. This larger pool has less international exposure and fewer personal sources of information than earlier generations of mobile students. This new group of students is looking for help and willing to pay for it. Universities now see these students as important sources of revenue as well as contributors to diversity. Competition for international students has increased greatly. As a result, new enterprises have appeared to address the demands of this growing market.

Recruitment agents are not new operators in higher education, and their participation in the university admissions process has always been controversial. The "agents" category often mixes individuals hired by universities to recruit students to the sponsoring institution with those hired by the student to help choose institutions to apply to and guide them through the admissions process, but there are important differ-

---

* With Liz Reisberg

ences. No data are available about how many companies or individuals engage in either activity, but their presence is growing and an increasing number of universities are using these services. For now all available information is anecdotal, since no research exists on this topic.

Recruitment Agents' Deeds

Recruitment agents typically serve as local salespeople for one or more universities overseas. They are *not* university employees; they are field recruiters. Their presence on the ground ensures that the institutions hiring them are more accessible to students interested in going abroad. They act as local promoters and a conduit of international applications for their university client(s). For this job they are typically paid a commission that ranges from 10 to 15 percent (but may go as high as 25%) of the first year's tuition, although some receive an annual fixed fee. The agents may but do not necessarily receive any professional training from their university clients, nor are formal mechanisms generally in place for keeping them current on programs or policies.

Agents may also act as guidance counselors, helping students sort through the overwhelming amount of information available on the Internet. However, their motivation does not consist of providing impartial information but rather to steer students to specific institutions—something that may not be entirely clear to a student who consults them.

The primary client for agents is the institution that hires them. In order to be successful, they must deliver an acceptable number of students to their sponsoring institutions. It is not known how frequently agents accept payment from students as well as universities and colleges, although anecdotal evidence indicates that this does happen. The key here is that the extent of their activities, source of their fees, and propriety of their services lack transparency, particularly to students.

It is not possible to confirm the extent of services provided, but they include activities required to match student clients with university clients. Many universities suspect that agents sometimes complete applications and write essays for their student clients. Although it is not possible to generalize, sufficient anecdotes have been reported to cause concern.

Other Information Sources

Another service available to internationally mobile students is offered by a growing number of private independent advisors. This service is hired by students to provide guidance in matching their goals, objectives, and academic profile to appropriate institutions overseas. Private consultants do not have contractual agreements with any university that would influence the advice they provide.

To be successful, these professionals must cultivate a local reputation for providing excellent service to students, not institutions; they must be well informed with current knowledge about a wide range of colleges and universities, academic programs, and admissions requirements throughout the world. They welcome contact with institutions, meet with traveling representatives, contact alumni, and often visit campuses abroad. In fact many universities seek out these advisors and provide them with information to share with their student clients; this "triangle" of communication works to everyone's advantage.

Also, advisors and extensive information are accessible to students in many countries at nonprofit advising centers operated by the British Council, the US State Department, and other governments and associations that provide a basic orientation to higher education in their respective countries and guide students to helpful resources. Yet, staffing at these agencies is inadequate to serve the growing international student market.

Perverse Incentives

The dynamic between an intermediary, an institution, and a student is inevitably influenced by the incentives and rewards that shape it. A recruitment agent's income depends on directing students to specific institutions. While this action may result in a good match for the student, the incentives are not set up to ensure the best match for the student or, for that matter, to work in the student's best interests.

Agents are entrepreneurs who earn their income from providing a service to two entities whose best interests may, or may not, be the same. The rewards arise from the relationship between the agent and the institution that hires him or her, not from the service provided to the student, presenting a potential conflict of interest that no professional standards or guidelines can eliminate. In fact, as long as the incentives favor the interests of the institution and agent over the interests of the student, professional standards will have limited effect.

No conflicting incentives exist for private consultants or nonprofit advising centers. The work is unambiguously directed toward the *best* interest of the student.

False Arguments and Lost Opportunities

Most of the arguments in defense of overseas agents appear somewhat hollow—such as, students cannot be expected to sort through vast amounts of data on opportunities abroad on their own; small institutions do not have staff or resources to launch effective international marketing campaigns; since agents are not going to take leave, standards should be set for their behavior; and the market will weed out unscrupulous recruiters.

Given the investment and consequences of the procedure, students should be required to participate actively in the research. It is too risky to have someone else make their decisions or even influence them, if the students lack the knowledge needed to judge advice fairly. It is inappropriate that a recruitment agent, motivated by economic gain, should be the source of all information.

While it is easy to commiserate with overwhelmed students who turn to agents for help, it is harder to sympathize with the inclination of institutions to do the same. International students enrich every campus, and hosting them requires a great deal of responsibility. When institutions work through agents, they sacrifice the benefits that result from the direct engagement of university administrators and faculty in recruitment, which ensures a necessary flow of information—about foreign cultures, foreign education systems, and international student needs. Similarly, direct communication with institutional representatives helps students receive accurate and up-to-date information.

Many alternatives are open to colleges and universities. College administrators can travel with a number of companies that organize international recruitment trips, at a range of costs; they can participate in overseas education fairs. Institutions with limited budgets have found creative ways to increase their visibility overseas and to reach out to potential applications. Numerous examples of recruiting successfully exist through students on study-abroad programs, faculty who travel, or combining efforts (and budgets) of multiple offices such as admissions, alumni relations, and development to send a single administrator abroad to represent the institution, Webinars (Web-based seminars) and other online events. Also, as mentioned above, many private consultants and advisors (professionals hired by students) welcome contact with international institutions.

Not knowing what agents actually tell their clients leaves students (and universities) very vulnerable. It is unrealistic to expect that "the market" will regulate quality or that unethical agents will be unsuccessful. The "market model" assumes that students (as consumers) have the knowledge and experience necessary to choose the best-quality service, and that is unrealistic. Adequate oversight is impossible, and professional certification will only provide "ethical cover" and a false sense of security to the institutions and students alike.

Conclusion

New enterprises have responded to opportunities that have arisen from growing international student mobility. Still, not all businesses that have found markets for their services should be welcomed. The use of recruitment agents by universities and colleges is clouded by many factors. Their activities cannot be adequately monitored to guarantee that student interests are protected. No international standards can guarantee local activity or that the relationship between an agent and a university will be entirely transparent to the student. Furthermore, the incentives and rewards do not depend on ethical behavior. One might also ask why, if the use of agents is forbidden in the United States for domestic recruitment of students, would it be acceptable for overseas recruiting?

Some universities do invest time and resources to ensure close communication with the agents they hire. Some are participating in a process to certify agents who adhere to ethical standards. Yet even then, ethical behavior is interpreted differently in various cultures. Who will provide the oversight and mediation to create compliance with standards as they are intended? By "outsourcing" recruitment, institutions are putting their reputation and vital communication with students to a third party, and this is a serious mistake.

A combination of good information available on the Web, the availability of impartial advice from experienced professionals and nonprofit agencies, and well-informed and user-friendly services by the host universities can address student needs. Paid recruiters are simply not necessary and, furthermore, work to the detriment of the process by standing between the direct exchange of information among students and institutions.

Perhaps most significantly, prospective students must take an active role in this research, ask good questions, and make informed decisions about where to study. Alumni of foreign universities can help them. The Internet is a good tool; visits to education information centers or education fairs can help; and direct contact with staff at prospective universities is essential.

There is no debate that agents are a strong presence in many countries. However, the issue of employing agents merits more public discussion, and it would be most unfortunate to forego the debate and proceed on the basis of "if you can't beat them, join them."

[*IHE* 63, Spring 2011]

28

Agents and Third-Party Recruiters in International Higher Education

A specter is now haunting international higher education—the dramatic proliferation of third-party recruiters and agents. Their job is to recruit prospective students in countries that send large numbers of students abroad to study at specific institutions as well as to provide general information about studying abroad. Many officials are authorized by academic institutions in the receiving countries—specifically in the United States, Britain, and Australia—to offer admission to students and facilitate their enrollment.

While by no means a new trend, this phenomenon is growing in size, scope, and notoriety, as international enrollments have become a compelling part of some universities' bottom lines. The operators, of course, do not work without any source of income. They are paid by the universities that utilize them, usually by providing a fee, based on how many students are enrolled. Sometimes, shockingly, they are also paid by prospective students.

This article has a simple argument that agents and recruiters are impairing academic standards and integrity and should be eliminated or severely curtailed. Providing information to prospective students is fine, but money should not change hands during the admissions process, and universities should not hand the power to admit—after all, a key academic responsibility—to agents or entities overseas.

Old Ways and a New Wave
Thirty years ago, most students interested in studying abroad would

locate information, apply to his or her preferred institutions, and enroll. In the days prior to the Internet, information could be obtained directly by writing to overseas universities or in some cases by going to libraries sponsored by embassies and information centers in major cities in the developing world supported by the main host countries—the Soviet Union, Britain, France, and the United States. Internationally mobile students were relatively few in number. In 1981, there were 912,300 internationally mobile students. The total has grown by three times in the past 30 years. Many students came from relatively sophisticated families able to access information and make informed choices or were sponsored by governments or other agencies. Universities in host countries seldom placed internationalization at the top of their agendas, and few, if any, looked to make money from overseas students. Cold War politics and neocolonial ties stimulated the major powers to sponsor information centers overseas.

This environment has changed. Indeed, practices only a few decades old seem quaint in today's globalized world, where higher education is big business for many and perhaps 3 million students study abroad—the large majority coming from Asia and going to the main English-speaking Western countries and Australia. The United States hosted 671,000 of these foreign students—or 21 percent of the global total. These students contributed more than $17.65 billion to the US economy and many billions more to the other main host countries.

The key shifts include the rise of the Internet, the commercialization of international study, the transformation of study abroad from an elite to a mass phenomenon. While formerly limited mainly to an elite few, participating students were often provided with scholarships from home or host countries. International study is now a mass phenomenon where funding comes overwhelmingly from individual overseas students or their families, and the students themselves come from much wider social-class backgrounds and from many more countries than was the case in the past.

The Internet permits easy access to information concerning higher education institutions everywhere, although even a cursory glance at the Web sites of many universities reveals a striking lack of transparency that even borders on false advertising. Even degree mills can be designed to look like Oxford—sometimes even stealing pictures of Oxford. But good information is available to individuals who have the ability to carefully separate fact from fiction—not an easy task.

The Cold War ended by 1990, and most host countries have eliminated or cut back their overseas information centers. Some, like Australia, have purposely commercialized international student recruiting. The Australian government established the IDP agency to build higher education as an export industry. Other countries, including the United Kingdom, have moved to commercialize international higher education.

At the same time, the United States has repeatedly cut the budgets for overseas libraries and information centers without thinking about the consequences and now faces the costly investment of reopening centers and libraries and rebranding and remarketing one of America's most valuable "exports."

As the number of overseas students has grown, the level of sophistication of the applicants has declined. At one time, fewer applicants were in large part interested in top universities overseas, although some government-sponsored programs placed students in less prestigious institutions. However, many of today's potential students have little knowledge about higher education prospects and may want to study abroad because they cannot find access at home. Moreover, they feel that somehow an overseas qualification will boost their job prospects or serve as a prelude to migration abroad.

Many more academic institutions have entered the competition for international students. Most of these new entrants are not top "name-brand" universities but are rather lesser-known—and sometimes lower-quality—schools of all kinds. These schools turn to recruiters since they feel that they have no alternative way to attract students from other countries. It is surprising that some quite respectable American universities have turned to agents and recruiters—perhaps feeling insufficient confidence that their quality and brand could attract overseas students. Top-ranked universities remain preferred destinations for the best and brightest students, but they can accommodate only a tiny minority of those who apply.

Agents and Recruiters Enter

This new environment produced an information and access vacuum that needed to be filled. Unfortunately, this deficiency has been accommodated in the worst possible way. Many universities, especially those with no international profile, seeking to attract international students find that they cannot easily obtain access to the potential market. Students find it difficult to locate reliable information about possible places to study amidst the thicket of competing Web sites and the myriad of advertisements that one can find in newspapers, train stations, and elsewhere in the developing world. The Internet has not solved the problem in part because it does not distinguish quality and provides unevaluated and unfiltered information. There is no way to easily evaluate the quality or veracity of information. Agents and recruiters have stepped into this environment of information overload and claim to provide a roadmap to the plethora of "information" currently available on the Internet and elsewhere.

The Actual Practices

If agents and recruiters only provided information, today's situation would not amount to a crisis. It would simply be problematical because the evaluation of the information would still be questionable. They are, of course, hired chiefly by potential host universities and other higher education providers to attract students to their institutions. Not information providers, the agents are salespeople. Their purpose is to sell a product, and they can use any required methods. They do not present alternatives or provide objective guidance to the potential applicants. Many of these operators—although it is not known how many—have authorization to actually admit students, often based on murky qualifications. Some of the least-scrupulous agents accept payment from both sides—their employing school or schools in the host country, as well as from the applicants—a clear violation of ethical standards. Most agents and recruiters are independent operators who have contracts with one, or more, overseas institution. The universities in the host countries that employ these personnel typically are the less-prestigious schools with little visibility overseas and often a tremendous financial need for foreign students to balance their own "bottom lines."

American federal law forbids payments to recruit domestic students. Thus, one wonders why it is appropriate, or even legal, for a university to pay agents to "import" international students whereas not domestic students.

Agents and recruiters have no stated qualifications, nor are they vetted by anyone. Efforts are now underway to create "standards" for this new "profession" but with no powers to either measure compliance or discipline violators. Organizations like NAFSA: Association of International Educators, the largest membership organization of international education professionals, accept these operators as members with no questions asked, thus giving an aura of respectability to them. Other groups, such as the American Association of Collegiate Registrars and Admissions Officers, have raised serious inquiries about their role. Current efforts to set standards and somehow "legitimize" agents and recruiters through a new organization called the American International Recruitment Council may be seen as too closely linked to them.

The Solution

The solution to this growing phenomenon is simple: abolish them. Agents and recruiters have no legitimate role in international higher education. They are unnecessary and often less than honest practitioners who stand in the way of a good flow of information to prospective students and required data about these students to academic institutions in the host countries.

Objective and accurate information and guidance are needed for both institutions and students. These sources can be provided through the Internet, preferably through Web sites with some "seal of approval" from a group of respected universities or an international or regional organization that has universal credibility. It would be helpful if countries that eliminated or cut back on information centers and libraries overseas could restore them. The cost is not high and the yield in goodwill, and reliable data would be immense. A significant role may exist for independent consultants who provide information and prepare students for the application process overseas but have no links and receive no money from the universities. Actually, a new organization, the Association of International Graduate Admissions Consultants, has been founded to establish and enforce appropriate standards relevant to this new role.

Universities in the host countries should immediately cease using agents and recruiters. Better and more useful information should be provided by universities themselves to more effectively inform prospective applicants. This goal may include visits by university admissions staff to potential students overseas for the purpose of information sharing.

The stain of commercialization in international higher education has been tremendously aided by agents and recruiters. It is high time that these operators are eliminated and replaced with open and transparent ways of providing information to prospective students. The admissions process should be put back where it belongs—students applying for study and colleges and universities choosing those best qualified— based on reliable individually submitted applications.

[*IHE* 62, Winter, 2011]

29

Academic Freedom: A Realistic Appraisal

Everyone seems to favor academic freedom. Indeed, if university leaders or ministers of education were asked, they would claim that this privilege is universally practiced. Yet, problems concerning academic freedom exist almost everywhere—created by changing academic realities, political pressures, growing commercialization and marketization of higher education, or legal pressures. The purpose of this article is to argue that academic freedom needs to be carefully defined so that it can be defended in the global climate of complexity. A new, and probably more delimited, understanding of academic freedom is needed in the age of the Internet and the global knowledge economy.

A Bit of History

Academic freedom has a long history in higher education but has always been contested by forces outside the university. Since the time of Martin Luther and Socrates, professors have been persecuted for their views— by state or religious authorities or by powerful interest groups who do not like dissenting views or uncomfortable truths. Modern academic freedom was perhaps first codified by Wilhelm von Humboldt when he developed the research university in Berlin in 1818. The German academic freedom idea was limited in scope. It included *Lehrfreiheit*—the freedom of professors to teach in their classrooms and to do research in the direct areas of expertise. The Humboldtian ideal did not include freedom to express views outside the professor's area of expertise and 19th century Germany often disciplined academics who expressed dissenting opinions about politics and excluded socialists or other dissenters from holding academic appointments. It should also be noted that students were guaranteed *Lernfreiheit*—the freedom to study what they wished.

The American Association of University Professors (AAUP) first focused on academic freedom in 1915, and its statement emphasized three main principles: "to promote inquiry and advance the sum of human knowledge," "to provide general instruction to the students," and "to develop experts for various branches of the public service." With the agreement of university presidents, the AAUP expanded the purview of academic freedom in 1940 to include professorial expression on topics outside of the direct academic expertise of the professor. In other words, professors had a wider range of freedom of expression, although the statement emphasizes professorial responsibility and recognizes some restrictions. In both the German and American cases, academic freedom included protection of academic appointments through a tenure system: professors could not be fired for their research or views on a range of topics. Professors came to be protected in roles as members of the academic community as well. They could not be disciplined because they might oppose university leadership on issues relating to academic governance of policy. This broader definition, stemming from both German and American traditions, seems to be widely accepted globally in countries that have a traditional commitment to academic freedom, although it is possible to point to many violations of the accepted norms.

Contemporary Confusion

At the same time, definitions about academic freedom are being expanded and contracted beyond generally accepted norms. Some now define academic freedom as virtually everything that permits effective teaching and research—faculty involvement in governance, adequate budgets for academic institutions, suitable conditions for teaching and learning such as appropriate classrooms and access to technology. This stretches academic freedom to include everything necessary for a successful university. At the other end of the spectrum, some countries or universities claim adherence to academic freedom where there are policies in place that restrict what can be taught in the classroom or on themes for research and publication.

Contemporary realities have also created complexities. The Internet, distance education, and related technological innovations, as well as the rise of multinational media conglomerates that increasingly control the distribution of knowledge, have raised questions about the ownership of knowledge. Issues related to academic freedom are involved in these technological debates.

Is academic freedom a necessary condition for high-quality "world-class" universities today? The evidence seems to show the requirement. The various international rankings of universities give those institutions with a high degree of academic freedom the top scores. Few highly ranked universities systematically violate traditional norms of academic freedom. A high degree of academic freedom is particularly important for the social sciences and humanities, but all fields benefit from freedom of inquiry and a sense that the university is committed to the free expression of ideas.

The Need for a New Consensus

Academic freedom is without question a core value for higher education. In the knowledge economy of the 21st century academic freedom needs some rethinking, with all of the pressures on higher education engendered by massification, commercialization, and accountability. What is needed is a return to the core concepts of academic freedom developed by von Humboldt and expanded in the AAUP's 1940 statement. Academic freedom, after all, is the right of professors to teach without constraint in their field of expertise, do research and publish, and express themselves in the public space (newspapers, the Internet, and so on). Academic freedom generally protects the employment of professors as well as providing the most ironclad guarantees possible—through a formal tenure or civil service system, or other arrangements.

A statement issued by professors at the University of Cape Town in South Africa and quoted in a famous 1957 United States Supreme Court decision states:

> It is the business of a university to provide that atmosphere which is most conducive to speculation, experiment and creation. It is an atmosphere in which there prevail "the four essential freedoms" of a university—to determine for itself on academic grounds who may teach, what may be taught, how it shall be taught, and who may be admitted to study.

These ideals neatly summarize many of the essential ideas of academic freedom.

Academic freedom does not essentially concern how universities are managed, whether they are adequately funded or even how the faculty is compensated. Academic freedom does not ensure that professors have a role in governance but should guarantee that they can speak out on internal management issues without fear of sanction. Academic freedom does not relate to accountability. Universities may legitimately demand appropriate productivity from faculty members. Professors' work may be evaluated, and inadequate performance may lead to sanctions or even, in extreme cases, firing, but only after careful procedures that do not violate academic freedom. Academic freedom protects professorial freedom of teaching, research, and expression—and nothing else.

Current Problems

Traditional academic freedom is under threat in many places today, creating the need for more attention to be paid to contemporary challenges. These crises range from professors being subject to severe sanctions for their teaching, research, or expression—including firing, jail, or even violence. Groups like Scholars at Risk provide assistance to such academics and publicize their problems. In some countries, restrictions exist on what can be researched, taught, and published. In some cases the restrictions are explicit, but in most cases the "red lines" that cannot be crossed are not clearly spelled out. Yet, academics may be sanctioned if they violate these terms.

The list of such countries and fields of inquiry is unfortunately rather long. In the United States, which has in general effective protections for academic freedom, problems are emerging. Courts have recently ruled that academics who speak out against the policies of their own universities and are penalized for such actions are not protected by academic freedom. The growing number of part-time teachers in many countries have no effective protection of their academic freedom, since they are often employed for just one course or for a short and often indeterminate period of time. The ownership of knowledge by multinational corporations or even by employing universities has become an issue of contention in some countries. Is it a violation of academic freedom for an external organization to control publication through ownership rights? Is academic freedom violated if governments impose curricular requirements of various kinds, as is the case in a significant number of countries? In short, academic freedom is under considerable stress today, and expanding the definition of this key concept to include basically everything makes the protection of the essentials of academic freedom increasingly difficult. The complexities of the 21st century require careful attention to the core principles of academic freedom so that they can be protected in an increasingly difficult environment.

[*IHE* 57, Fall 2009]

30

"Meddling" or "Steering": The Politics of Academic Decision Making in Hong Kong*

The latest flap in Hong Kong's contentious world of higher education concerns the unwillingness of the government-appointed council of the Hong Kong Institute of Education to reappoint Paul Morris as president. The Hong Kong academic community sees this action as a severe violation of academic freedom—the latest in a number of high profile cases over the last decade where government authority has tried to limit academic freedom by putting pressure on the universities and their top leaders to silence or remove professors who were perceived as disconcerting or obstreperous. But is this case a matter of academic freedom? However loyal to President Morris the academic community may be—and however unwelcome the nonreappointment may be—it is nonetheless important to provide an accurate analysis.

Academic freedom, after all, relates to guarantees of free expression for professors and students. The original 19th century German definition of academic freedom was limited to such protection within the classroom and laboratory in fields of the expertise of the professor. It did not protect expression on other topics. In the early 20th century, Americans expanded the idea of academic freedom to guarantee expression on any topic and in any context. Academic freedom protected the jobs of professors. They could not be fired or disciplined because of

* With Gerard A. Postiglione

their writings or expression, on campus or off. This expanded definition of academic freedom is by and large accepted everywhere—that is, where academic freedom is respected. Academic freedom does not assure that professors will control the university, nor does it protect institutional autonomy. Academic freedom does not insulate either professors or institutions from accountability accessible to those who provide funding and who, through legal arrangements, control institutional decisions.

Thus, the charge of restricting academic freedom may not be justified. Morris has pointed out that he had to protect the autonomy of academic staff to express their views publicly. This differs from a Hong Kong University case in 2000 when an institutional head succumbed to government pressure and unsuccessfully (as alleged) set a process in motion to silence a professor.

The Morris crisis relates to the alleged desire of the government to merge the Hong Kong Institute of Education with the Chinese University of Hong Kong. Morris supporters attribute the nonrenewal of his contract to resisting a merger. The academic freedom of staff was not limited by government, and no member of the Hong Kong Institute of Education staff was fired or disciplined for expression of views.

An International Perspective

The government provides most of the funding for higher education in Hong Kong and has the legal power to determine broad policy directions. In Europe, such power is called "steering" and is subject to considerable debate. As European academic systems expanded, governments, which fund higher education, took increasing control over how these growing systems are organized. Internal academic management remains mainly in the hands of the academics, but demands for accountability of academic performance are slowly changing the equation. The United Kingdom is a good example of how a state has exercised increased authority—measuring academic performance, imposing increasing fees on students, and the like. The academic community has had little impact on these policies, often unsuccessfully opposing them.

In the United States, colleges and universities have always been subject to the control of boards of trustees or regents. In general these boards have no academics on them, which is why they are called "lay boards." These boards appoint presidents and other top administrators and determine institutional policy. Presidents serve, as the saying goes, "at the pleasure of the board." A year ago, Harvard's board, called the Corporation, lost confidence in President Lawrence Summers. He quickly resigned. This same group just appointed Harvard's first female president, Drew Gilpin Faust. The faculty did not remove Summers nor did they elect the new president. Most American universities have a system of shared responsibility for policy. Academics determine key internal matters, including having a voice in the appointment of top administrators. Lay boards, which in the public universities are generally appointed by government authorities, are the main arbiters of the direction of the institution.

Many in the academic community worldwide argue that academic staff should have a large measure of control over their universities. Academic institutions, before the age of mass higher education, did have a significant measure of institutional autonomy. But since massification, the power of the academic community to shape the destiny of their own universities and of higher education in general has been diminished. The impact of marketization, the expansion of universities into giant bureaucracies, demands for accountability, and related forces have revolutionized the internal management of universities and how decisions concerning the direction of academic systems are made.

Academic Freedom or Not?

Definitions make a difference. If this latest crisis in Hong Kong's academic life is in fact a matter of governance and control rather than academic freedom, the attention should be placed on what is the proper role of the Hong Kong government in "steering" the academic system. Should the academic community and the leaders of the institutions have a significant role in shaping academic policy? If so, how should a shared governance arrangement be organized? Alternatively, should universities and their academic staff be treated like the employees of any company or government? We are convinced that the pendulum has swung much too far in the direction of government authority and managerial power, to the long-term detriment of the strength of the system.

[*IHE* 47, Spring 2007]

31

The Asian Higher Education Century?

The 2009 world university rankings showed a modest increase in the number of universities in Asia that have entered the top 100—in the Shanghai Academic Ranking of World Universities from 5 to 6, and in the *Times Higher Education*/QS rankings from 14 to 16. Commentators immediately referred to the academic rise of Asia and a concomitant decline of the West. Fundamentally, however, academic excellence, research productivity, and reputation, which are mainly what the rankings capture, are not a zero-sum game. The improvement of universities in one part of the world does not mean that institutions elsewhere necessarily decline. Further, the shift to Asia is by no means dramatic. It is in fact a good thing that universities outside the traditional powerhouses of North America and western Europe are improving and gaining increased recognition for their work.

Nonetheless, it is useful to examine Asia's academic growth if only because the region houses the most rapidly expanding economies in the world, and a number of Asian countries have placed great emphasis on both expansion and improvement in higher education. While it is almost impossible to generalize about so vast and varied a region, nonetheless some realities are relevant for significant parts of the region.

Asia is home to a majority of the world's private higher education institutions, and the private sector continues to expand in the region. With a few exceptions, the private sector stands at the bottom of the prestige hierarachy. As the economists put it, the private academic institutions are "demand absorbing" and provide access but generally not high quality. The private sector does not contribute much to the improvement of the quality of Asian higher education.

Asia has a significant high-quality sector. Many Japanese universities are highly ranked. Singapore and Hong Kong have excellent academic systems. Outstanding universities exist in South Korea and Taiwan. China's top dozen or so universities are approaching "world class." The Indian Institutes of Technology, although not universities in the traditional sense, are also top institutions. But overall, Asia's universities do not compare favorably with those in North America, western Europe, or Australia. A number of structural, academic, and cultural factors may inhibit even some of the best Asian universities from rising to the pinnacles of academic quality in the near future and are likely to some extent inhibit the improvement of Asia's universities in general.

Asian strategies for academic improvement differ. Singapore and Hong Kong have accomplished considerable success simply by building Western universities in Asia by hiring large numbers of nonlocal academic staff, using English, and copying Western norms of academic organization and management. South Korea has sponsored several national campaigns for academic upgrading such as the Brain Korea project. Taiwan has relied in part on convincing Western-educated Taiwanese to return home to improve key universities that have been given extra support. Singapore has strategically invited several foreign universities to open branches and has given them significant financial incentives to do so—although several have failed.

China's efforts have been the most impressive: a combination of significant infusions of funds to universities identified as top performers, mergers to create institutions with both high quality and economy of scale, and efforts to create an academic environment that rewards productivity.

It is possible, however, that in China and elsewhere in Asia a kind of "glass ceiling" will soon be reached. Financial and other resources combined with some innovative strategies can make progress only so far. Cultural, academic, and historical challenges persist and may well slow the upgrade of Asian universities. The rise of Asian higher education is by no means inevitable, at least in the near future.

Major Impediments

An academic culture that is based on meritocratic values, free inquiry, and competition—combined with elements of collaboration and at least some mobility—is central to a world-class university. There is some recognition of the importance of these elements in much of Asia and of the difficulties of implementation and impediments based on historical tradition and other forces.

Relationships are, of course, essential everywhere and in all institutions and societies. But in Asia, personal connections and networks—the

Chinese call it *guanxi*—are still influencing many aspects of academic life, from the admission of students to the promotion of professors and the allocation of research funds. One implication is widespread inbreeding of faculty. Those trained at a university are hired by that institution and typically spend their careers there. This may hinder new thinking and innovation because of common perspectives and an undue respect for academic hierarchy. It may also often be difficult to encourage innovation in this environment. The ties between a former student and his or her mentor might shape departmental or institutional politics and inhibit change or foster factionalism.

Many Asian universities have a combination of affinity-based promotion policies for academic staff while simultaneously lacking a formal "tenure" system. As a result, many persons appointed to an academic position are in due course promoted without much careful evaluation. Furthermore, many systems in this part of the world do not provide formal protection of academic freedom or a promotion policy that rewards productivity and encourages long-term performance.

Teaching and, to some extent, research often follow quite traditional methods and emphasize lectures with little interaction between students and professors. Professors often simply repeat their lectures and leave little if any time for questions or discussion. Much criticism has been produced concerning traditional teaching in recent years, with a recognition that it does not contribute to either long-term learning or independent thinking. These methods extend to graduate education, as well, where formality is often the rule, and independent "hands on" work is still not the popular norm.

Hierarchy is very much at the center of academic ties of all kinds. This often means that students are inhibited from the kinds of informal interaction with their teachers as enjoyed by counterparts at Western universities. Junior staff are subject to the methodological and topical constraints of senior professors. Key academic decisions are often in the hands of more experienced professors and are related to the Asian respect for age and to the nature of many Asian societies, although some top universities have rapidly promoted younger professors and have hired a large number of foreign-trained staff.

Academic corruption exists, at least to a limited extent, everywhere, but the problem seems to be endemic in some Asian countries. Reports concerning favoritism in admissions to plagiarism in publication, and falsifying research findings can be found regularly in many Asian newspapers. A study by China's Wuhan University estimated that $100 million is spent annually for ghostwritten academic papers by academics and students. One of the world's top medical journals, Britain's *Lancet*, warned that China will not become a research superpower by 2020 as promised by President Hu Jintao, unless academic fraud is more tightly controlled. Few statistics are available, but anecdotal evidence indicates the problem is fairly widespread, even in some top Asian universities.

In most Asian countries, graduate education is at a relatively early stage—in need both of expansion and of shaping effective programs to provide a research base for Asian universities and the ability to educate the next generation of professors and researchers. Typically, professors who focus their work on postbaccauleareate education tend to be the most research active. Their academic responsibilities emphasize research and the training of small numbers of graduate students. Even many of Asia's best universities provide more emphasis on undergraduate programs—thus making the emergence of research universities more difficult, although some top institutions, for example in China, have dramatically expanded graduate programs.

Internationalization is widely recognized as a necessary part of any top university. Many of Asia's universities have stressed it, but the adversities are significant. What should represent the balance between the local language and English, as the main language of scientific communication? In some universities, professors are encouraged to publish in major international journals—not an easy task in the highly competitive arena of science and scholarship. Some classes are taught in English, but at times with mixed results. The complex issues relating to branch campuses, franchised degree programs, and involvement with foreign universities are multifaceted and not always beneficial for the Asian institutions. Most of the world's internationally mobile students come from Asia, and many do not return home following their overseas study—although this trend is slowly changing.

The final impediment is the academic profession—at the heart of any university but especially important for a top "world-class" university. For many Asian countries, the professoriate is inadequately paid in comparison to local salaries and woefully remunerated by international standards. Teaching loads are often too high to permit much research to be performed. In many countries, academics are promoted because of longevity rather than for merit. Another challenge is the lack of a tenure system that provides firm guarantees of academic freedom. Professors need both better job protection and more money and at the same time a competitive environment to ensure high productivity.

The Future of Asian Universities
While it is very difficult to generalize about Asian countries, some generalizations are possible. Most countries in Asia—with some notable

exceptions in Japan, South Korea, Taiwan, and Singapore—are still rapidly expanding enrollments. Thus, competition for public funds for rapidly expanding systems is intense. Top-tier universities often lose out in the struggle for resources. The growing private-sector institutions have no interest in research and will not produce prestigious universities.

Several Asian countries have undertaken ambitious plans for improving higher education, and some are making impressive progress. China, South Korea, Singapore, and several others have invested heavily in higher education, with the top universities improving significantly. Other countries—notably India, Indonesia, Vietnam, and most of the poorer Asian countries—have a very long way to go.

While there has been impressive progress in some Asian countries and in some sectors of academe, many obstacles remain to achieve world-class status. The struggle is a long one and will require not only resources but also changing deeply entrenched academic practices. But building world-class universities is necessary for Asia to continue its impressive economic progress. Sophisticated research capacity and highly skilled people are needed for Asia's future.

[*IHE* 59, Spring 2010]

32

The Humanities and Social Sciences in Asia: Endangered Species?

Most observers agree that the humanities and social sciences—the soft sciences—are an integral part of any university, indeed that a real university must have strength in these areas. These disciplines are important in their own right, and are a central core for any general education program. The humanities and to a lesser extent the social sciences are in crisis in many East Asian universities. Few students are choosing to focus their studies on the humanities—fields such as philosophy, history, and cultural studies. Linguistics and language studies, other than practical English programs, are also in decline. The social sciences, particularly such disciplines as economics and a few others that relate to management or policy studies, fare somewhat better. A conference held recently at Harvard University and sponsored by the Harvard-Yenching Institute brought together leaders of key East Asian universities and Harvard scholars to examine the "crisis of the humanities and social sciences" in East Asia.

A "Perfect Storm" of Problems for the Soft Sciences

Many universities, in a rush to become "world class" by emphasizing the hard sciences and other easy to quantify disciplines, have let the soft sciences languish. As governments and universities worldwide have emphasized the "private good" aspects of higher education more than the "public good," universities and public funders generally support fields that will yield income or that are in student demand. The traditional public good roles of universities—providing education in all branches of knowledge, cultural analysis and critique, the integration of science and culture, and the preservation of knowledge—have been largely pushed aside. Students find that the sciences and especially professional fields such as management and law provide more secure and remunerative careers, causing enrollments in the humanities and some of the social sciences to plummet. Jobs outside academe are easier to obtain and more remunerative with training in professional fields and the sciences; even within academe, salaries are higher in these fields. The rise of private universities—the fastest-growing sector in higher education worldwide and the dominant force in such East Asian countries as Korea, Japan, Taiwan, and the Philippines—has meant in some cases an emphasis on fields that are in high student demand.

Mass higher education brought immense pressures on higher education systems everywhere and has been particularly damaging for the soft sciences. First generation university students typically choose fields that will yield easy employment after graduation—seldom the soft sciences. Budgetary pressures caused by massification meant reduced funding for fields not in high demand.

The Soft Sciences and General Education

Most East Asian universities, as is common worldwide, provide a specialized curriculum with a vocational or disciplinary focus, and students must enroll in specific faculties. General education is, by and large, absent, although exceptions do exist—such as the University of Tokyo, which requires a year of general education. A reconsideration of this specialized professional curriculum has recently begun, with critics arguing that it stifles creativity and forces students to confine the focus of their studies. Moreover, the specialized curriculum may be irrelevant for the more fluid job market of the 21st century.

As the idea of general education and an interdisciplinary approach to the curriculum strengthens, the role of the humanities and social sciences becomes more central. General education never provides an exclusively science-based curriculum, and in most cases the soft sciences are at least as significant as the hard sciences and professional subjects. With declining strength in the soft sciences, the development of innovative and effective general education programs will be difficult if not impossible.

A related concern in many East Asian universities is the development of critical thinking skills as part of the academic curriculum. As with general education, any innovative effort in this direction must involve the humanities and social sciences.

Current Realities

With enrollments down and funding cuts, humanities programs have been reduced or even eliminated. In countries such as Japan and Korea, private universities that traditionally stressed the soft sciences are in jeopardy because of enrollment declines in a difficult demographic environment. Fewer doctorates are being produced in most of these disciplines, reflecting student preferences; fewer academic positions are available; and salaries have not kept up with other fields. The professoriate is aging and often not being replaced.

At the same time, a new recognition that the soft sciences are needed to support academic programs exists—as well as a growing concern to ensure critical thinking for first-degree students and in fledgling general education courses.

Challenges

Ensuring appropriate strength in the humanities and social sciences is complex. Both academic institutions and government must recognize that the soft sciences are important for the university—and funding made available. Some academic departments of high quality that can produce top humanities and social science scholars are a basic necessity. Not every university needs to have the capacity to produce doctorates, but the system must. Unlike some fields in the hard sciences, where it does not matter where a scientist is trained, advanced education in the humanities and some social sciences fields at home is in most cases valuable because the national context is important and expertise is unlikely to exist abroad. In such fields as national and local history, national culture and language, and related subjects, local expertise as well as sources and documentation is often quite good at home. In academic systems that value foreign degrees, this may place the humanities at a disadvantage.

The humanities particularly are often relegated to a distant and low prestige part of the university. The soft sciences must regain their places at the center of academic life. These fields must themselves reintegrate into the mainstream of the university by emphasizing interdisciplinary work, their contributions to general education, and their importance to understanding contemporary society. New fields such as bioethics and environmental science, if they are to be effective, need significant expertise from the humanities and social sciences. Business programs require a strong element of the social sciences and the best ones include a consideration of ethics. Too often, humanities scholars are content to stick to their narrow disciplines—they must convince others of the relevance of their expertise. If general education and creative thinking are to become part of the curriculum, expertise in the humanities and social sciences is absolutely necessary.

Several key challenges are evident: to improve the image of the soft sciences at every university; to provide capacity in a country to educate scholars at a high level in the various soft science disciplines (all universities of course not need to offer a full range of specialties); to integrate the humanities and social sciences into interdisciplinary programs in professional and other fields; and to have capacity in these fields to contribute to general education.

The humanities and social sciences are not only an essential part of the idea of the university; they are at the core of understanding contemporary society. History, sociology, philosophy, and other disciplines interpret today's key challenges. The university, as the central institution providing careful analysis and interpretation of society, requires the soft sciences as never before.

[*IHE* 52, Summer 2008]

33

Chinese Challenges: Toward a Mature Academic System

Cross-border academic engagement is never an easy process. Cultural, administrative, curricular, and often political differences must be understood—and effectively considered in any successful collaboration. This article focuses on the complexities and some of the challenges of an expanding and developing Chinese academic system. To paraphrase Mao Zedong, the academic system is the ocean in which all academic collaboration swims.

Unprecedented Expansion

China's academic expansion in the past several decades has been unprecedented. In 1978, only 1.5 percent of the age cohort attended higher education. By 2010, the proportion had increased to 27 percent and is estimated to expand to 36 percent by 2015. China's higher education system is now the largest in the world, with more than 31 million students enrolled, the majority of whom attend tertiary nonuniversity institutions. The growth of a new private higher education sector has also been unprecedented. There are now more than 800 "nonstate" (private) higher education institutions, enrolling more than 4 million students.

This expansion, while extraordinarily impressive, has created some problems. Dramatic growth, combined with diffuse responsibility for higher education among ministries at the national, provincial, and municipal levels and now shared with the private sector, has created considerable confusion about goals, mission, and funding. While there have been efforts to create a differentiated academic system that identifies specific missions for institutions, considerable confusion remains. Further, a wave of institutional mergers and combinations, undertaken to create more comprehensive universities and improve quality, has yielded mixed success.

China has been most successful in building its research university sector—by injecting massive resources through the 985 Project. These government-funded initiatives identified about 40 universities throughout the country and provided funding and other support to enable some of them to build world-class facilities and recruit the best professors and students. Perhaps a dozen of these universities are likely to compete with the best institutions worldwide, for talent and prestige. An additional initiative, the 211 Project, provided supplementary funds to an additional 120 universities.

It is, however, fair to say that much of the rest of the system is without direction and often starved for resources. Most universities strive toward a research mission, even if they lack the appropriate staff or financial resources. Many universities borrowed heavily from state-run banks, to build their campuses, and face unsustainable debts that cannot be repaid. The quality of many institutions toward the bottom of the Chinese academic hierarchy is questionable, and graduates of these institutions are finding it hard to obtain a job.

Much of the new private sector is problematical. Only a small minority of the *min ban* (people run) nonstate postsecondary institutions is authorized by the Ministry of Education to award academic degrees. Others provide certificates of various kinds. Quality varies tremendously, and many institutions are simply trade schools focusing on specific vocational fields, while most are for-profit.

The Future of Expansion

China faces an uncommon problem. On the one hand, enrollment will significantly rise in the coming decades, as China fulfills its goal of educating 40 percent of the age cohort by 2020. It is estimated that 36 million students will study in postsecondary institutions, which will require continued expansion. At the same time, China's demographic profile is changing. For example, the population of 18- to 22-year-olds peaked in 2008 at 125 million, but will decline to 88 million by 2020. Postsecondary enrollments will continue to increase, because of the expansion of access. However, the rapid building of facilities that characterized the past few decades will no doubt decrease.

Currently, the access bottleneck seems to be at the top universities, where competition for entry is fierce, and all of the well-qualified students cannot be accommodated. Thus, a growing number of the brightest Chinese students, who might otherwise remain in China if seats at top institutions were available, are going abroad for undergraduate study. Those who have lower scores on the *gaokao* (national entrance examination) may find it easier to attend a university—but harder to locate employment upon graduation.

The Academic Profession

Professors are the core of any university. The Chinese academic profession faces significant problems. One-third of academic staff nationally hold only a bachelor's degree—the proportion increases to 60 percent in the new private sector. At the top universities, at least 70 percent of the faculty has earned a doctorate. Academic salaries are low—with the exception of a small percentage of highly productive academics at top universities. Chinese academics do not earn enough to live a middle-class style and must moonlight—that is, accept additional teaching responsibilities on campus or, otherwise, find additional income. In a recent study of academic remuneration in 28 countries, China scored lowest when measured by purchasing power parity measures. There is also a good deal of inbreeding in faculty hiring and a considerable use of guanxi (personal connections and networks), as well.

Governance

Chinese universities are highly bureaucratic, and the concept of shared governance is limited. Senior professors seem to dominate internal decision making. Senior administrators are for the most part appointed by top management but usually with input from relevant departments or schools. The dual management system constitutes a president, with the main responsibility for academic affairs, and a party secretary (now often called the chairman of council), with control over budget, ideology, internal management, and promotions. The party secretary is appointed by provincial or national authorities. Top Chinese universities are moving slowly toward shared governance arrangements more familiar in the West.

Building an Academic Culture

Effective universities need a vibrant academic culture. Most Chinese universities are still developing such a culture, although the top universities are making significant progress. The elements of an effective academic culture, generally taken for granted in the developed world, remain a challenge in many other parts of the world. Indeed, for China to develop truly world-class universities, the development of key elements of academic culture is required. Otherwise, a kind of glass ceiling is likely to be reached.

Some of the central elements involve a full commitment to academic freedom—so that scholars and scientists are free to publish and communicate as they wish, particularly in areas of their academic specialty. Unfettered access to information via the Internet as well as in books and journals is also a requirement. The university in all of its functions must be both meritocratic and reasonably transparent. This means that personal, political, and institutional connections must not influence decisions regarding personnel, research, or other academic matters. The academic environment must be free of plagiarism, cheating on examinations, and other elements of corruption. All of these issues remain problematic in many sectors of Chinese academe. Efforts are being made to curb such practices, but they remain ingrained in the system.

Conclusion

Universities and academic systems worldwide face an array of 21st century challenges. China's higher education institutions are not exempt to contemporary turmoil. As an expanding postsecondary system still in the process of building both enrollment capacity and academic quality, China's challenges are different from those facing the developed world. Yet, problems exist, and foreign institutions seeking to engage with China's expanding academic system must fully understand these realities, when considering possibilities for engagement.

[*International Briefs for Higher Education Leaders* 1, 2012]

34

Chinese Higher Education in an Open-Door Era

China is opening its doors to foreign higher education providers at a time when competition and markets are being expanded domestically. Today, about 1,400 foreign higher education institutions have been approved by various education authorities in China to operate in the country. This large number brings both promise and peril. The opportunity to bring new academic ideas and practices into the country may also be interpreted as a powerful invitation for problems and crises.

As Chinese higher education is being increasingly deregulated internally, the Ministry of Education is permitting foreign providers to operate. Many Chinese universities face financial shortfalls and thus explore new ways of generating revenues. Among these new market ideas are linkages with foreign providers—the thought being that an overseas connection will bring prestige, a sense of cosmopolitanism, and perhaps some new educational concepts. The central government, provincial and municipal authorities, and university administrators have all embraced internationalization for many reasons—the most important of which are commercial benefits and the need to provide access to those seeking a postsecondary degree.

Foreign Motivations and Programs
China's expanded freedom of access coincides with a growing interest in China by other countries. Again, the main foreign motivation is commercial, but there are mixed rationales from abroad. Universities worldwide see China as a major market—for recruiting students

to study abroad, for "buying" some of the brightest Chinese scientists for academe and industry, and now for exporting educational programs and institutions. Chinese policymakers and institutions should remember that while foreign partners' own purposes and motives may often coincide with Chinese interests, it is possible that sometimes they might not.

Foreign institutions and governments have other motivations as well. A few foreign universities have strong historical links to China, and their motives are mainly academic. For examples the Hopkins-Nanjing master's program has been operating for more than two decades, and the ties between the prestigious American Johns Hopkins University and Nanjing University ensure strong academic values and quality. Similarly, a longstanding linkage between a consortium of American Jesuit universities and Peking University in the area of business studies has produced joint degrees and a strongly collaborative curriculum. Other foreign universities are interested in providing a place for their own students to study in China—to learn about language, history, and culture, as well as to provide direct experience in a rapidly changing Chinese academic, social, and business environment. These programs are part of the internationalization strategy of many American and European universities.

Most foreign academic institutions are interested in China as a "market" for their educational products. They sell degrees, curricula, and other educational programs, often in partnership with Chinese institutions. They also offer opportunities for Chinese students to study abroad. Now, with fewer restrictions placed on foreign educational entrepreneurial activities in China, the scope of foreign activities will expand and will include foreign branch campuses.

Who Comes?

While there has been no accurate census of foreign educational providers in China, it is possible to make a few generalizations. Most of the foreign academic institutions interested in the "China market" are not the top institutions in their own countries. Further, the prestigious foreign schools tend to link up with the most prominent Chinese universities in metropolitan areas, while the others mostly focus on provincial areas. At the top end, Yale and Cornell in the United States and several Australian institutions are now working in China with a variety of motivations—including providing opportunities for their own students and faculty to learn about China, expanding their "brand" to the Chinese market, and recruiting top Chinese students and staff to their home campuses.

For the United States, many of the lower-prestige colleges and universities tend to collaborate with smaller provincial institutions in China—precisely those institutions that have a minimal understanding of the complex US academic marketplace and hierarchy and little knowledge of their partners. The US institutions, for their part, want to earn money while providing a useful educational program. In Australia and to some extent the United Kingdom, universities have been told to recruit international students and establish overseas academic partnerships and branches to earn income to make up for reduced government allocations. Foreign institutions generally provide academic programs that are inexpensive to set up and operate and can quickly attract a local market willing to pay for the product. Business management, information technology, and related fields are particularly popular for these reasons.

The Japanese experience with foreign transplants may be useful. In the 1980s, a number of mostly lower-tier American colleges and universities entered the Japanese market at the invitation of local governments or institutions in provincial parts of the country. When these US schools found that recruiting local students was more difficult than anticipated and that the Ministry of Education was not so friendly, they pulled out of the country. Without question, if most foreign partners find that the Chinese market proves difficult in terms of earning money or for operational reasons, they will withdraw as quickly as they entered.

Accreditation and Quality Assurance

In the United States, almost all academic institutions are accredited by the nongovernmental US regional accrediting agencies. While these accreditors are quite effective and respected by the higher education community and government authorities, they do not provide any assessment of quality. They provide a basic floor of academic performance below which an institution cannot go and still receive accreditation. Thus, many unimpressive institutions, including some in the new for-profit sector, do receive accreditation. In much of the world, quality assurance is at an early stage of development, and it generally provides a fairly basic assessment of performance. Thus, Chinese reliance on the mechanisms will provide only an assurance that foreign institutions do not fall below a rather modest standard. Further, some current efforts to provide international quality assurance standards may serve the interests of those providing higher education services rather than those at the receiving end.

What To Do?

China needs to carefully consider the new influx of academic institutions and programs. It is a mistake to simply open the door wide and hope that the "market" will take care of any problems that might occur. Chinese national needs, the "common good" as a major goal for higher education, and quality assurance need protection in any foreign academic relationships.

The General Agreement on Trade in Services (GATS) of the World Trade Organization, currently being negotiated as part of the WTO Doha round, can have significant implications for China. GATS proponents seek to force countries to open their doors to foreign academic institutions and programs from abroad. It is in China's interests to ensure that its national needs are kept in mind and that China, at least in the foreseeable future, has only a small export market for its educational programs and institutions.

It is not at all clear that accredited but low-quality foreign colleges and universities are serving students or the Chinese academic system well. There should be a working system to evaluate foreign academic institutions seeking to enter China—including a thorough assessment of quality and an understanding of the position of the institution in its home environment. Such an arrangement, set up by Chinese researchers or with assistance from objective foreign experts, could help to evaluate potential foreign partners. Singapore, for example, has developed a list of overseas institutions considered appropriate for government-sponsored scholarships or other collaborative higher education programs.

Consideration should be given to the institutional motivations as well as the terms and conditions of any agreements with foreign partners or schools desiring to work in China. Is a foreign institution offering its best quality programs and staff? Is there appropriate accountability for performance? Do the programs offer more than the prestige of an international linkage? Is staff and institutional development part of the agreement? What is the "business plan" of the foreign provider? Questions need to be asked to ensure that the best interests of the host institution and the students are well served.

It is likely that in some cases local institutional or government authorities may fail to adequately examine overseas collaborations or may lack the expertise to make appropriate judgments. National or at least provincial agencies should have authority to review overseas programs. The review process should be as transparent as possible.

Decisions concerning foreign academic relationships or granting permission to foreign institutions to operate in a country are important.

They have significant implications for the local higher education community—a good partner can bring new ideas and good quality education. An ineffective link may be costly to host institutions. And perhaps most relevant, students may not be well served. China is not alone in facing difficult decisions concerning foreign academic relationships. India, Malaysia, South Africa, and other countries find themselves in similar circumstances in an increasingly globalized world of higher education. Despite an internationalized environment, higher education remains a key responsibility of nations to supervise to ensure that their national interests are served and both access and quality are preserved.

[*IHE* 45, Fall 2006]

35

India's Higher Education Challenges

India's higher education achievements since independence in 1947 are impressive. With some 21 million students enrolled in postsecondary education, India has the third-largest higher education system in the world and is about to overtake the United States and become number two—although it serves approximately 18 percent of the age group. Continued expansion is inevitable. Further, higher education institutions are located throughout the country, including in many rural areas. India, through its various "reservations" (affirmative action) programs, has been able to provide access to disadvantaged students. Without question, the higher education system—and particularly the world-renowned Indian Institutes of Technology—has educated the brains that fueled India's impressive technology development, as well as a significant part of Silicon Valley.

Yet, on the whole, India's higher education system suffers from a quality deficit, is poorly organized, overly bureaucratic, lacks direction, and does not yet serve a large-enough proportion of young people demanding access. This article takes a "glass half empty" approach in order to highlight the challenges facing India's higher education future. Those wishing to interact with India's colleges, universities, and research institutes need to have a realistic picture of the country's dynamic yet troubled higher education environment.

A Pattern of Inadequate Investment
Higher education has never been adequately funded. In 2011/12 India spent a modest 1.22 percent of its gross domestic product on postsecondary education—a more modest investment than some other rapidly

expanding economies and well below European levels of expenditure. Much of this expenditure comes from students and their families, through tuition payments, rather than from the state. From the beginning, emphasis was placed on meeting the demands of mass access and expansion, rather than building up a meaningful high-quality university sector; and even financial support for mass access has been inadequate.

Gigantic and Poorly Organized

It is estimated that half the world's postsecondary institutions are in India—more than 34,000 undergraduate colleges, 174 universities, and in addition 12,748 diploma-granting entities. In most cases, undergraduate colleges do not have the authority to grant their own degrees; they must be "affiliated" to a university that supervises the curriculum, examines students, determines entrance requirements, and ultimately awards degrees. To some extent the affiliating system provides quality control but also eliminates autonomy from the colleges. As Pawan Agarwal points out in his article in this *Brief*, the affiliating system prevents innovation. Of the universities and other degree-awarding institutions, 152 are centrally funded and most of them do not have colleges to supervise—these tend to be the best ones. One-hundred-thirty additional institutions hold "deemed" status; and they are recognized by governmental authorities to grant degrees. These vary from low-quality private universities to top-quality specialized institutions in a variety of fields, from fundamental research in the sciences to management schools.

A variety of governmental entities have authority over higher education. Higher education is a shared responsibility of the state and central governments, but most funding comes from India's 28 states. The states have varying policies and differing abilities to provide financial support. Few of the states have coherent policies concerning postsecondary education. The central government sponsors 40 universities and 112 other prominent institutions—such as the Indian Institutes of Technology, the Indian Institutes of Management, National Institutes of Technology, and others—among these the best in India. The central government funds innovation, much of the country's research, and has some control over standards. The University Grants Commission, for example, funds innovation and has some regulatory responsibility. The All-India Council for Technical Education has authority over the nonuniversity postsecondary technical institutions. There is a veritable alphabet soup of central (i.e., national-level) agencies providing various kinds of support to higher education. This shared responsibility often leads to a lack of coordination, duplication, and complex bureaucratic requirements.

In part, as a result of this lack of clear authority and planning, India has no higher education "system." All of the universities are free to compete for resources and seek to develop a research mission, even if this is impractical. At the same time, most of the undergraduate colleges are prevented from innovating because of their tight administrative controls.

Politicization

Significant segments of Indian higher education are highly politicized. Colleges and universities are, in much of the country, coveted local institutions. They have significant budgets and offer employment to many—from professors to janitors to tea-wallahs. Thus, local and state political authorities want to control academic budgets, staffing decisions, and other aspects of academic life. Politicians like to establish colleges in their districts as sources of patronage. Academic life, in many colleges and universities, is also politicized. Academic appointments, election to governance bodies, and other decisions are sometimes influenced by local or party politics.

An Increasingly Dominant Private Sector

India's higher education system has always been a curious, and perhaps internationally unique, combination of public and private institutions. Almost from the beginning, most undergraduate colleges were established by private interests and managed by private agencies—such as philanthropic societies, religious groups, or others. Most of these private colleges received government funds and thus were "aided" institutions. The universities were all public institutions, for the most part established by the states.

This situation has changed dramatically in recent years. Most of the private colleges established in the past several decades are "unaided" and thus fully responsible for their own funding through tuition charges or other private sources of funds. Some "in demand" colleges, particularly in medicine and health professions, charge "capitation" fees—up-front payments to secure admission. Similarly, many of the "deemed to be universities" are also private institutions—receiving no government funds. Some of the unaided colleges and universities seem to be "for profit," although management and governance is often not very transparent. Most, although not all, are in the lower ranks of the academic hierarchy. The unaided private colleges are affiliated to a university in their region, and it is increasingly difficult for the universities to effectively supervise the large number of colleges, particularly when the financial aspects of the institutions are not obvious. There is also a small but growing number of mainly nonprofit private institutions moving toward offering high-quality and usually specialized higher education.

Conclusion
India has, without doubt, a functioning higher education establishment, which is characterized by, as India's new Minister of State for Education Shashi Tharoor has noted, both a "sea of mediocrity" as well as significant "pinnacles of excellence." The basic challenge is to improve the sea while supporting the pinnacles. This will require a lot more resources, new ideas, and a commitment to both access and excellence.

[*International Briefs for Higher Education Leaders* 3, 2013]

36

Getting Value for Money in Higher Education[*]

Although Indian higher education suffers from many dysfunctionalities and the system overall is characterized by "pinnacles of excellence in a sea of mediocrity"—by some international comparisons, India does reasonably well. Here are a few examples:

- India is a global leader in terms of gross domestic product (GDP) spent by public and private sources on higher education. India devotes a very high proportion of its national wealth of higher education. At 3 percent of the GDP (1.2% from public and 1.8% from private sources), Indian spends more than what the United States (1.0% public and 1.6% private) or Korea (0.7% public and 1.9% private) spends on higher education. This suggests a limited scope for further increase, although more is required since in absolute figures investment in higher education does not measure up in international terms. Further, there is an urgent need for effective and efficient use of funds, in order to promote both equity and excellence.

- India's gross enrollment rate, 18 percent, the proportion of the age group accessing higher education, is among the highest of countries at India's level of development. This is particularly impressive given India's size and complexity. The recently approved 12th Five-Year Plan aims at raising the gross enrollment rate to 25 percent by 2017 and is both desirable and achievable.

* With Pawan Agarwal

- Finally, academic salaries, when measured against other countries by accurate purchasing power parity comparisons, are quite good. Among 28 countries in a recent study, India ranked fourth from the top in entry salaries for academics—and better than the other BRIC (Brazil, Russia, India, and China) nations. China scored near the bottom for average salaries. This good showing is the result of the major pay increase implemented in 2006.

Value for Money?

Is India gaining value for its investment in higher education? Also, is more money the answer to the challenges? Most observers would agree that on average Indian colleges and universities do not produce a very distinguished job and are definitely not "world class." A number of factors are related to the positive trends noted here. Although India invests significant sums in postsecondary education, with the funds increasingly coming from students and their families, it does not spend effectively. There is little coordination between the states and the central government.

Many of India's 34,000 undergraduate colleges are too small to be viable. They are generally understaffed and ill-equipped; two-thirds do not even satisfy government-established minimum norms, and they are unable to innovate because of the rigid bureaucracy of the affiliating system that links the colleges to a supervising university. All this makes the system highly fragmented, scattered and difficult to manage. There is a strong case for consolidation and merging small institutions. But the affiliating system is vast and deep-rooted and, therefore, is neither feasible nor desirable to dismantle it. However, decentralization of part of the curriculum holds great promise. With greater academic autonomy, the core courses could be retained by the university, while the responsibility for the rest of the curriculum could be devolved to the colleges. This would create a desired innovation culture in the colleges. Clustering and even merging colleges that are very small would also have to figure into this reform. In addition, universities that affiliate a large number of colleges would need to be reorganized into two or more universities, with each of them affiliating a smaller number of colleges—in order to improve overall academic effectiveness.

While gross enrollment rates are not bad by relevant international standards, India, however, is about four decades behind most advanced nations in enrollments. While the United States had an enrollment rate of 15 percent by the 1940s, most advanced nations reached that stage several decades later. The United Kingdom, Australia, France, and Japan had enrollment rates of 18, 23, 24, and 25 percent in 1975;

and Korea enrolled only 8 percent in 1975, which rose to 13 percent in 1980, and then rapidly rose to 34 percent in 1985. All these countries have achieved a system close to universal higher education; but it must be recognized that enrollments have grown hand in hand, based on the rise in demand for qualified people with agriculture contributing to less than 5 percent of the workforce. Considering that over half of the people in India are still engaged in the farm sector with limited need for higher qualifications, current levels of enrollment in India appear to be adequate. The bigger challenge is that the students do not choose to study in fields that will best contribute to economic growth—or to their own job prospects. Also, employers regularly complain that graduates are not adequately for available jobs.

While it is true that Indian academics, by international comparisons, are relatively well paid, they are not necessarily effective. Academics, and especially college teachers, are constrained by rigid bureaucracy. Further, their work is not carefully evaluated—salary increases and promotions are awarded rather on the basis of seniority. Unfortunately, when salaries were increased in 2006, this boon was not accompanied by any reforms in the teaching profession or requirements for evaluation. A System of Academic Performance Indicators for promotion and appointment of professors and lecturers is yet to take roots. It appears that Indian academics want to do a good job and most are committed to their profession—structural impediments and an ossified culture get in the way.

Our general impression is that despite several areas in which India compares well, globally, deep structural and cultural impediments constrain the academic system as a while from performing effectively.

Conclusion
India has achieved some areas of accomplishment in higher education. The challenge is to capitalize on these plans and reform an ossified system. In the Indian case, expenditure does not necessarily mean effectiveness. In this way, Indian higher education may be compared to the American health care system. The United States spends the most per capita on health care, but expenditure does not yield results. The Obama reforms, like the 12th Plan India, may finally improve an ossified system traditionally dominated by special interest and conflicts between the federal government and the states. The recently approved 12th Plan provides a good framework for change. It seeks to align central government investment with that of the state governments—align new capacity with demand. It also seeks to create a performance culture through deepening of competitive grants and creation of related

institutional arrangements. However, success depends on effective implementation.

[*IHE* 72, Summer 2013]

37

India's Effort to Join 21st-Century Higher Education*

India's central government will create 12 new central universities, adding to the 18 that currently exist. This is a mammoth undertaking—Rs. 3,280 crores (about $73 million) has been allocated from the central government budget to it. Earlier in the year India announced it will create 30 "world-class" universities, 8 new Indian Institutes of Technology (IITs), and 7 Indian Institutes of Management (IIMs) in the coming five years. On the recommendation of the National Knowledge Commission, the central government is planning massive investment to upgrade and expand higher education. Other plans include enhancing the salaries of college and university academics—boosting salaries by as much as 70 percent.

This prospect represents welcome news since India currently lacks world-class universities according to the international rankings, and Indian academics, when compared internationally, are rather poorly paid. Students also suffer an immense shortage of places in India's top academic institutions and throughout the higher education system. India today educates only half as many young people from the university age group as China and ranks well behind most Latin American and other middle-income countries.

India exhibits a special problem at the top of its higher education hierarchy. With the notable exceptions of the IITs and IIMs, and a small number of outstanding nonuniversity research and training institu-

---

*With N. Jayaram

tions—such as the All India Institute of Medical Sciences—top-notch schools are rare. Indeed, none of India's 348 universities are ranked in the top 100 in the world. Generally, when India has wanted to innovate in the higher education sector, it has sidestepped the universities and has started entirely new institutions such as the IITs.

However, if India invests large amounts of money and human capital into academic improvement and expansion without undertaking strategies to ensure that the investment will yield results, resources will be wasted and failure will be assured. Despite a discussion of organizing some of the new university based on the American model, so far neither the ideas nor the funding seems adequate. Yet, a newspaper reported that one official said: "The view was that there should be no hierarchy or disparity in standards amongst universities, and the reforms and changes suggested for world-class universities should be applied to all universities." This attitude shows a complete misunderstanding that the American system institutes significant hierarchy among the public universities.

Just pumping money and resources into a fundamentally broken university system is a mistake. Establishing new universities, especially those intended to be innovative, requires careful planning and an understanding of the weaknesses of the current system. Let us outline some of the problems that need fixing before resources are given.

Bureaucracy Without Accountability
India is world famous for sclerotic bureaucracy, and higher education fits into that mold. Few decisions can be made without taking permission from an authority above, and the wheels of decision making grind slowly. Fear of corruption or of a loss of control entrenches bureaucracy. Teachers and academic leaders at colleges and universities have little incentive to innovate higher education—indeed quite the opposite. It is completely impossible to build world-class universities in this bureaucratic context. If the new institutions must tolerate responsibilities to both the central government and the states in which they are located, the bureaucratic burden will be completely overwhelming.

Location
Great universities need to be located on friendly soil. In general, the best universities worldwide are in or near major urban centers or in places with intellectual traditions and strength. While it is entirely appropriate to have a good university in each of India's states, the idea of a truly world-class university (an institution that can compete with the best universities in the world) in cities like Guwahati or Bhubanesh-

war is simply unrealistic. It would be extraordinarily difficult to attract top professors or even the best students, and the "soft" infrastructures, such as most cultural amenities, are missing. High-tech industry is also absent in these locations and would be difficult to lure. No amount of money will guarantee the establishment of a world-class university in such places.

The Academic Profession

Indian academics deserve higher salaries, and the current move to dramatically improve remuneration is a positive step. It would be a serious mistake to simply give more money to the professoriate without at the same time demanding significant reforms in the structure and practices of the profession. Indian academics are rewarded for longevity, rather than productivity, and for conformity rather than innovation. The most productive academics cannot be rewarded for their work, and it is almost impossible to pay "market rates" to keep the best and the brightest in the universities. World-class universities require a salary structure that rewards productivity.

Academic Culture and Governance

Indian universities are enmeshed in a culture of mediocrity, with little competition either among institutions or academics. Universities are subject to the whims of politicians and are unable to plan for their own futures. Academics are seldom involved in the leadership and management of the universities. Bureaucracy governs everything and holds down innovation. Without essential and deep structural change in how universities are governed and in the culture of the institutions, there is little possibility for improvement. An additional challenge is that some of the world-class universities are to be created by improving existing state universities. This will be extraordinarily difficult, since these institutions are, with very few exceptions, mired in mediocrity and bureaucracy, and hardly amenable to change and improvement, even with the carrot of additional resources.

An element of corruption exists at many levels of the higher education system, from favoritism in admissions, appointment to faculty positions, exam cheating, questionable coaching arrangements, and many others. Damaging at all levels, corruption destroys a research culture and makes a world-class university impossible.

Meritocracy at All Levels

World-class universities are deeply meritocratic institutions. They hire the best professors, admit the most intelligent students, reward the brightest academics, and make all decisions on the basis of quality. They reject—and punish—plagiarism, favoritism in appointments, or corruption of any kind. Much of Indian academe, unfortunately, does not reflect these values. Some of the problem is structural. The practice of admitting students and hiring professors on the basis of rigid quotas set for particular population groups—up to 49 percent—however well intentioned or justified, virtually precludes meritocracy. Deeply ingrained in Indian society and politics, the reservations system may well be justified—but to have successful world-class universities, meritocracy must be the primary motivating principle.

The Role of Research
World-class universities are research intensive. All highly ranked universities in the world exhibit this characteristic. India faces several problems in developing a research culture. It is fair to say that no Indian university today is, as an institution, research intensive. India's universities can claim a small number of departments that have a high level of research—and many highly accomplished professors work in the system. And some institutions, such as the IITs and some nonuniversity agencies like the Tata Institute of Fundamental Research and the All India Institute of Medical Sciences, produce impressive research and are respected internationally. The creation of a research-intensive university is mandatory to achieve world-class status.

Resources
Rs. 3,280 crores for the 12 new central universities, plus the other impressive amounts announced for related projects, sounds like a lot of money. In fact, it is very inadequate. Creating a world-class research university that can play in the best international leagues is an expensive undertaking—to establish and then to sustain. As an example, one large research-intensive new Chinese university cost around $700 million to build and has a total annual budget of close to $400 million.

Conclusion
The challenges facing the creation of world-class universities are daunting. Indeed, if India is to succeed as a great technological power with a knowledge-based economy, world-class universities are required. The first step, however, is to examine the problems and create realistic solutions. Spending large sums in a scattershot manner will not work. Nor will copying the American academic model succeed.

[*IHE* 54, Winter 2009]

38

The Achilles Heel of India's High-Tech Future: World-Class Universities

Ten thousand American expatriates are now working in India for high-tech companies. Infosys and Tata Consultancy Services, the Indian high-tech giants, will together hire and train more than 50,000 college graduates from abroad, including more than 1,000 from the United States, in the coming year. Why? Because Indian universities are not producing the quality graduates needed for the top end of the new economy. India produces many university graduates—in 2004 there were almost 700,000 degrees granted in science and engineering alone. However, with few exceptions, the institutions themselves are not of high quality. According to recent international rankings, only the Indian Institutes of Technology are noted at all, and even these are not anywhere near the top of the charts. It is not quantity, but rather quality that is lacking.

India does not spend enough on higher education—only 0.37 percent of GDP. The United States spends 1.41 and the United Kingdom 1.07 percent. Only countries such as Japan and Korea, where more than 80 percent of students are in largely unsubsidized private universities, approach India's low spending levels. China spends considerably more than India.

India has never seriously cared about the quality dimension of higher education. All countries are faced with the dilemma of catering to mass demand while at the same time maintaining and enhancing quality.

India has consistently supported access over quality. There has been no recognition that all modern nations must have a differentiated academic system, with an elite sector at the top, mass-based and less selective institutions in the middle, and vocationally oriented postsecondary schools at the bottom. Patterns of funding, government support, and management will necessarily vary. At the top, the research universities aspire to the highest international standards of quality, follow a meritocratic code, and are ready to compete with the best universities worldwide.

The Current Debate

The tiny quality sector in Indian higher education is now being severely undermined. The new policy, introduced by the government without consulting the academic community, has been hotly contested and overwhelmingly opposed by the higher education community. The policy will increase the proportion of places reserved for lower-caste economically disadvantaged groups at India's small number of top institutions will make it impossible for India to develop internationally competitive "world-class" universities. Government policies, when implemented, will mandate awarding more than half the seats in entering classes to disadvantaged groups. However laudable the goal of lessening social inequality, this policy destroys international competitiveness at the top institutions. The problem involves not only the specific reservations and the ideology behind them but also the effect on the meritocratic ethos of the research universities and other elite institutions such as the institutes of technology and management. It also leads to such absurd consequences as students with zero scores on admissions tests being admitted and the creation of two distinct sets of students in the same class, with an adverse impact on teaching and learning. If India wishes to play in the international big leagues and to economically compete in a globalized world, it will need higher education institutions that prepare graduates to function in this environment, conduct advanced research that serve to advance the Indian economy, and participate at the top levels of international science and scholarship.

What Is Needed

For a start, there must be a recognition that elite higher education is necessary. A small part of India's higher education system must function at the upper international levels—as elite institutions in the best sense of the term. This does not mean that the entire system should be elite. Serving the needs of mass access and social mobility for disadvantaged groups is important, but it is not the only goal of higher education.

India is now wealthy enough to support both educational goals.

Research universities everywhere have some common characteristics.

- *Meritocratic values.* A meritocratic university seeks to hire the most qualified faculty members, enroll the brightest students, and reward both students and staff for top performance. Fairness and consistency are central supports of academic meritocracy.
- *Governmental support.* Almost everywhere, research universities are public institutions. Even in the United States, where some research universities are private, they received significant government support for research. In India, only the government has the resources to support research universities. Funding must be consistent and sufficient to support a vibrant research agenda. Research universities cannot be built on the cheap.
- *Internationalization.* Research universities are by their nature international institutions, linking with other similar universities in other countries and participating in the international scientific community. India has the advantage of its use of English, the world's language of science, and its possession a large group of academics who have received training at the best universities abroad. India must take steps to broaden its international reach.
- *The public good.* Research universities serve the interests of society, and they require public support. They should not be forced to engage exclusively in applied research and to pay for themselves by charging high tuition and producing income from all research activities. An effective mix of basic and applied research is needed. Scholarship funds for needy but able students are also required to supplement tuition fees.
- *The academic profession.* Top-quality professors are central to the success of a research university. Professors must be adequately paid so that they can devote their full-time attention to academe, and so that the "best and brightest" can be attracted to the profession. There must be a stable, and competitive, academic career path that rewards merit and productivity—and punishes poor academic work by ejecting those unable to adhere to the highest standards.
- *Research and teaching.* Research universities emphasize and reward top-quality research, but they are also teaching institutions. Both research and teaching are necessary and contribute to the institution's goals.
- *Autonomy and accountability.* Research universities require a significant degree of autonomy—more than they have traditionally had in India's highly bureaucratic environment. At the same time, accountability is needed to ensure effective performance.

The Indian Institutes of Technology are a uniquely Indian contribution to higher education. While they are not quintessential research universities, they play a key role in India's elite higher education sector. The must be supported and strengthened as institutions that support India's high-tech development.

Conclusion

India is truly at a turning point. If the nation is to fulfill its economic and technological potential in the 21st century, it must have an elite and internationally competitive higher education sector at the top of a large and differentiated higher education system, with a mixture of public and private support. The elite sector requires support and recognition. It cannot afford being used as a tool for partisan political policies. World-class research-oriented universities are the spearhead of India's international competitiveness.

[*IHE* 44, Summer 2006]

39

Kerala: The Dilemmas of Equality in Higher Education[*]

One of India's smaller states offers some interesting lessons concerning higher education and its role in development as well as alternative approaches to higher education policy. The state of Kerala, on India's southwest coast, is unusual in the Indian context. The state's social and political circumstances have contributed to its higher education development. Kerala has a population of 31 million, with an unusual religious mix by Indian standards—one-quarter Christian, one-quarter Muslim, and about half Hindu. It may be a useful case not only for India but for other developing countries.

While not wealthy even by Indian standards—it ranks ninth in gross domestic product among India's 28 states—Kerala is by most measures the most advanced state in India in education. It has universal literacy and enrolls around 18 percent of the age group in postsecondary education, double India's average and almost on a par with rapidly developing China. Women constitute more than 60 percent of the total higher education enrollment—the highest in India. The state also boasts the highest Human Development Index rating in India, with the highest life expectancy and the lowest infant-mortality rate.

Politically, Kerala also represents an interesting case. Its current government is a coalition dominated by the Communist Party of India (Marxist). The communists, who have been in power off and on since the 1950s, have in many ways shaped modern Kerala's society. Kerala

* With Eldho Mathews

was the first state in the world to actually elect communists to power. Early on, they were able to push through meaningful land reform and have emphasized social services, education, and income redistribution. An active media keeps debate lively and helps to promote transparency and a high degree, by Indian standards, of probity in government. Everyone seems to belong to a union—including university and college teachers, students, and campus workers. One vice chancellor said that one of her main jobs was keeping track of and consulting with unions. Most of the population seem to be represented by some organization, thus giving a voice to much of the population.

The vast chasm between rich and poor, so evident in India and much of the developing world, seems much less obvious in everyday life in Kerala. Corruption seems less endemic and social relations, in general, more stable.

Kerala missed out on India's "industrial revolution." Perhaps industries were leery of the well-entrenched unions. This means that the pollution of the environment common elsewhere is largely missing in Kerala—the state's informal motto is "God's Own Country"—an effort to build up Kerala's successful tourist industry. There is also not much of an economic base—agriculture and the fishing sector remain important, as does tourism, and also the export of skilled personnel, especially to the Gulf countries. Here, Kerala's high levels of literacy and its well-educated population have contributed to the attractiveness of its world force. Almost a quarter of the state's gross domestic product comes from the remittances of overseas workers. Policymakers are now fostering "technoparks" in the hope of making the state attractive to India's burgeoning information-technology sector; the first technopark was established in Thiruvananthapuram, the state's capital in 1990. Yet, Bangalore is currently the major hub for information technology companies and is India's "silicon valley," and Kerala is struggling to catch up.

Higher Education in the Mix

Kerala shares India's higher education problems but has tried with some success to ameliorate them. The "affiliating" system ties undergraduate colleges to universities that set examinations, impose a variety of rules, and regulate them. The University of Kerala, one among the first 16 universities established in India, is the state's premier institution. It has 198 affiliated colleges that educate around 100,000 students. Some of these colleges are located as far as 140 kilometers from the university campus. A majority of the colleges are private and managed by a variety of religious, social, and other nonprofit organizations. Many are "aided" and receive government funds; they tend to be the better ones in terms of infrastructure and facilities. The growth in recent years of private colleges, mainly in such fields as medicine, engineering, information technology, nursing, and management studies that receive no government funding—many of which are quasi-for-profit—has created problems for the university authorities as they are asked to provide affiliation to institutions that may be of questionable quality. Nearly half of the affiliated colleges—a total of 797 in the state—are controlled by private managements, mainly sponsored by the Christian or Muslim minority communities or individuals belonging to these communities.

Facilities at most of the colleges and in the university departments as well are well below international standards, often with outdated laboratories and rudimentary information technology facilities and inadequate libraries. In addition to supervising the colleges, the universities provide postbaccalaureate instruction. All postsecondary education in the state is in English.

Kerala's Higher Education Policies

The state's approach to higher education is somewhat unique in the Indian context. Most higher education in the state was at one time supervised and funded by the state government. However, this situation has been changing, especially during the last decade. Resource crunch and budget constraints have forced the universities to change priorities. While India's central government has with a few exceptions ignored Kerala, given its commitment to sponsor at least one central university in each of India's states, the government plans are proceeding to build a central institution in a rather isolated location in the northern part of the state. This development is not understood by most higher education experts in the state, since it is unlikely that such an institution located far from academic or urban centers can succeed.

In keeping with its egalitarian philosophy, the government has provided generally equal support to all of the universities and has not identified any as a "flagship." Thus, there are few nationally or internationally prominent universities in the state. One exception is the Cochin University of Science and Technology. The central Ministry of Human Resource Development recognized the university's excellence and supported upgrading it to the level of the Indian Institutes of Technology. However, a campaign against the conversion of the university into an IIT forced the authorities to shelve the plans. The Indian Institute of Space Science and Technology has been recently established by the central government in Thiruvananthapuram. The Sree Chitra Tirunal Institute for Medical Sciences & Technology, Thiruvananthapuram, is another exception; this institution has the status of a university and offers post-doctoral, doctoral, and postgraduate courses in medical specialties and health care technology and is under the administrative control of the Department of Science and Technology, Government of India. Indian Institute of Science Education and Research, Thiruvananthapuram, established in 2008, can also be considered a nationally prominent institution. It is an autonomous institution affiliated to the Ministry of Human Resources Development. As a matter of policy, Kerala might be well served if these institutions were closely linked or even merged so as to combine these high-quality institutions and produce a world-class scientific institution in the state.

Several of the arts and sciences undergraduate colleges that have a long historical tradition—such as University College in Thiruvananthapuram, the capital, or Maharaja's College in Kochi—are able to attract a number of bright students. But these institutions' facilities are far from world class. However, most of the top students prefer professional courses in engineering, medicine (which is an undergraduate subject area in India), and business. Currently there are 96 engineering colleges in Kerala. Almost 90 percent of them had started functioning during the last decade, and only 11 of these colleges are government sponsored. Of the 96 colleges, 60 of them are purely private institutions. In general, their facilities are no better than the average found in the state.

Kerala has instituted a few significant reforms—changes suggested by national authorities but not initiated widely so far. These innovations include a semester system and reforms in the traditional undergraduate examinations. The idea is to provide better assessment through more frequent examinations and evaluations tied more closely to course content. This reform required significant changes in the way the curriculum was organized, how courses are taught, and how they are assessed. Policymakers hope that it will result in improvements in teaching. The Higher Education Council was set up to provide advice to the state government, conduct research on higher education issues, and serve as a forum for discussion about higher education. The central government recommended that all of the states organize such agencies, but so far only a few states have done so. The council does not have the power to implement reforms and only makes recommendations to government and the universities.

Kerala, like all of the states, is grappling with the rapid and largely unregulated expansion of new private colleges and specialized postsecondary institutions. On the one hand, there is a need for greater access, and these new private colleges provide this. But on the other, many of them are of dubious quality, operate on the edges of quality control, and are largely organized to earn a profit for the owners. They serve high-demand fields such as management, information technology, and related technical fields. A few are medical colleges. So far, a good deal of grumbling about these institutions has taken place but little action to control them.

Although an increase in the number of higher education institutions and student enrollment over the last two decades has taken place, inequalities based on the quality of primary and secondary schooling have been on the rise during this period. One of the most observable effects of this change is in the relationship between type of schools attended and admission to professional colleges. This trend is evident in the outcome of medical-engineering entrance examinations conducted by the government. Entrance to the medical and engineering colleges in Kerala is largely based on an entrance examination conducted by the government every year. However, students from the Central Board of Secondary Education affiliated schools and Council for the Indian School Certificate Examinations affiliated schools have a better chance to bag the top ranks of this examination. Most of these schools are in the unaided/for profit sector. However, more than 80 percent of the higher secondary students in the state are pursing studies in postsecondary institutions affiliated to the Directorate of Higher Secondary Education of the Government of Kerala.

The majority of the top-rank holders of the entrance examination for professional programs emerge from the middle and upper strata of the society. The parents have the financial capacity to send these students to entrance coaching centers. This has created a situation in which the entry routes to higher education are differentiated on the basis of wealth. Coupled with this, personal and parental choices have become an important feature of Kerala's higher education. Students and parents these days are quite conscious about the inseparable link between academic choice and careers. The emergence of a new middle class in Kerala society accentuated this phenomenon. Naturally, this period witnessed an increase in the number of self-supporting students from Kerala going abroad to study.

A Way Forward

Kerala quietly has provided acceptable-quality higher education, by Indian standards, to a remarkably large part of its population. It has implemented several meaningful reforms in recent years, and higher education remains an issue of concern for the government and the public at large. A few policy initiatives may be useful to further improve the system.

The state's higher education institutions are largely similar in quality, focus, and funding. With the few exceptions noted here, none of these stand out either within the state or nationally. A mass higher education system needs to be differentiated—with institutions serving different missions, patterns of funding, and quality. Kerala needs at least one "world-class" university—an institution that can attract the best students in the state, be recognized as among the top universities in India, and gain visibility abroad as well. This strategy will not be easy since Kerala has a strong tradition of egalitarianism, but it is a necessary policy if the state is to fully participate in the global knowledge society of the 21st century. It is likely that the University of Kerala, perhaps merged with several high-profile scientific institutions located in the capital, is the logical choice, probably along with the Cochin University of Science and Technology. This does not mean that the other universities can be neglected. Some will focus largely on teaching and serving their specific regions, while a few, perhaps those focusing on science and technology, can retain some research mission.

In common with all regions of India, the large number of colleges affiliated to universities need to be appropriately supervised but at the same time permitted leeway to start innovative programs and achieve a degree of autonomy. A special problem concerns the growing number of new private "unaided" colleges, a majority of which are for-profit. Perhaps an effective accrediting system, supervised by the Higher Education Council or some other governmental body, could provide a basic standard of quality for all of the colleges and remove some of the burden from the universities.

Kerala's universities have the potential of jump-starting the state's move into the knowledge era. They can provide the training needed for a new generation of professionals ready to work in information technology and other knowledge industries. Kerala has the disadvantage of starting late. The giant info-tech superpower in Bangalore, for example, is far ahead—even though the first "technopark" in India was established in Thiruvananthapuram. But Kerala has a well-educated workforce, a tradition of hard work, and an ability to collaborate with people from many different backgrounds. An important step would be to immediately improve the quality of engineering education. The info-tech companies estimate that only one-fifth of engineering graduates can be immediately put to work; the rest need additional training. If Kerala can provide an engineering education that can produce engineers who can be immediately put to work without expensive further education, it will immediately improve its prospects for luring high technology to the state. Moreover, these graduates will be quite competitive on the international job market as well.

The state's higher education future is complex but practical. Expansion will continue, although the pressures may be somewhat less than in other parts of India because of Kerala's impressive access rates. Careful attention needs to be given to the organization of the higher education system. Some additional funds are required to transform at least one university into a research-intensive institution, while at the same time supporting a better-defined differentiated higher education system.

[*IHE* 61, Fall 2010]

40

India's Open Door to Foreign Universities

India may finally open its doors to foreign higher education institutions and investment. The cabinet has approved human resource development minister Kapil Sibal's proposed law, and it will be voted in Parliament in the near future. Indian comment has been largely favorable. What will an open door mean for Indian higher education—and to foreign institutions that may be interested in setting up shop in India? Basically, the result is likely less than is currently being envisaged, and there will be problems of implementation and of result as well.

The Political and Educational Context

Everyone recognizes that India has a serious higher education problem. Although India's higher education system, with more than 13 million students, is the world's third largest, it only educates around 12 percent of the age group, well under China's 27 percent and half or more in middle-income countries. Thus, it is a challenge of providing access to India's expanding population of young people and rapidly growing middle class. India also faces a serious quality problem—given that only a tiny proportion of the higher education sector can meet international standards. The justly famous Indian Institutes of Technology and the Institutes of Management constitute a tiny elite, as well as a few specialized schools such as the Tata Institute of Fundamental Research, one or two private institutions such as the Birla Institute of Technology and Science, and perhaps 100 top-rated undergraduate colleges. Almost all of India's 480 public universities and more than 25,000 undergraduate colleges are, by international standards, mediocre at best. India's complex legal arrangements for reserving places in higher education to members of various disadvantaged population groups, often setting aside up to half of the seats for such groups, places further stress on the system.

A Capacity Problem

India faces severe problems of capacity in its entire educational system in part because of underinvestment over many decades. More than a third of Indians remain illiterate after more than a half century of independence. On April 1, a new law took effect that makes primary education free and compulsory. While admirable, it takes place in a context of scarcity of trained teachers, inadequate budgets, and shoddy supervision. Minister Sibal has been shaking up the higher education establishment as well. The University Grants Commission and the All-India Council for Technical Education, responsible respectively for supervising the universities and the technical institutions, are being abolished and replaced with a new combined entity. But no one knows just how the new organization will work or who will staff it. India's higher education accrediting and quality assurance organization, the National Assessment and Accreditation Council, which was well-known for its slow movement, is being shaken up. But, again, it is unclear what will take its place or how it might be changed.

Current plans include the establishing of new national "world-class" universities in each of India's states, opening new IITs, and other initiatives. These plans, given the inadequate funds that have been announced and the shortage of qualified professors, are unlikely to succeed. The fact is that academic salaries do not compare favorably with remuneration offered by India's growing private sector and are uncompetitive by international standards. Many of India's top academics are teaching in the United States, Britain, and elsewhere. Even Ethiopia and Eritrea recruit Indian academics.

This lack of capacity will affect India's new open-door policy. If India does open its door to foreign institutions, it will be unable to adequately regulate and evaluate them.

Why Welcome the Foreigners?

Minister Sibal seems to have several goals for permitting foreign universities to enter the Indian market. The foreigners are expected to provide much needed capacity and new ideas about higher education management, curriculum, teaching methods, and research. It is hoped that they will bring investment. Top-class foreign universities are anticipated to add prestige to India's postsecondary system. All of these assumptions are at the very least questionable. While foreign transplants elsewhere in the world have provided some additional access, they have not dramatically increased student numbers. Almost all branch campuses are small and limited in scope and field. In the Persian Gulf, Vietnam, and Malaysia, where foreign branch campuses have been active, student access has been only modestly affected by them. Branch campuses are typically fairly small and almost always specialized in fields that are inexpensive to offer and have a ready clientele such as business studies, technology, and hospitality management. Few branch campuses bring much in the way of academic innovation. Typically, they use tried and true management, curriculum, and teaching methods. The branches frequently have little autonomy from their home university and are, thus, tightly controlled from abroad. While some of the ideas brought to India may be useful, not much can be expected.

Foreign providers will bring some investment to the higher education sector, particularly since the new law requires an investment of a minimum of $11 million—a kind of entry fee—but the total amount brought into India is unlikely to be quite large. Experience shows that sponsoring universities abroad seldom spend significant amounts on their branches—major investment often comes from the host countries such as the oil-rich Gulf states. It is likely that the foreigners will be interested in "testing the waters" in India to see if their initiatives will be sustainable, and thus are likely to want to limit their initial investments.

Global experience shows that the large majority of higher education institutions entering a foreign market are not prestigious universities but rather low-end institutions seeking market access and income. The new for-profit sector is especially interested in global expansion as well. Top universities may well establish collaborative arrangement with Indian peer institutions or study/research centers in India, but are unlikely to build full-fledged branch campuses on their own. There may be a few exceptions, such as the Georgia Institute of Technology, which is apparently thinking of a major investment in Hyderabad.

At least in the immediate and midterm future, it is quite unlikely that foreign initiatives will do what the Indian authorities hope they will accomplish.

The Half-Open Door

India's open door comes with a variety of conditions and limitations. It might better be called the "half-open door." These conditions may well deter many foreign institutions from involvement in India. The proposed legislation requires an investment of $11 million up front by a foreign provider in the India operation. Moreover, the foreign provider is restricted from making any profit on the Indian branch.

It is not clear if Indian authorities will evaluate a foreign institution before permission is given to set up a branch campus or another initiative—or if so, who will do the vetting. It is not clear if the foreign branches will be subject to India's highly complicated and controversial reservations regime (affirmative action programs) that often stipulates that half of enrollments consist of designated disadvantaged sections of the population. If the foreigners are required to admit large numbers of students from low-income families who are unlikely to afford high foreign campus fees and often require costly remedial preparation, creating financially stable branches may be close to impossible.

A further possible complication may be the role of state governments in setting their own regulations and conditions for foreign branches. Indian education is a joint responsibility of the central and state governments, and many of the states have differing approaches to higher education generally and to foreign involvement in particular. Some, such as Andhra Pradesh and Karnataka in the south, have been quite interested. Other states—such as West Bengal with its communist government, may be more skeptical. And a few, such as Chattisgarh, have been known to sell access to university status to the highest bidders.

Foreign institutions will need to deal with India's often impenetrable and sometimes corrupt bureaucracy. For example, recent reports have evidence that some Indian institutions were granted a coveted "deemed" university status after questionable practices between the applicants and high government officials. It is unclear if the foreign branches will be evaluated by Indian authorities or if overseas quality-assurance and accrediting agencies will be fully involved.

In short, many unanswered questions remain concerning just how foreigners will be admitted to India, how they will be managed, and who will control a highly complex set of relationships.

A Likely Scenario

India's higher education needs are significant. The country needs more enrollment capacity at the bottom of the system as well as more places at its small elite sector at the top. The system needs systemic reform. Furthermore, fresh breezes from abroad might help to galvanize local thinking. Yet, it is impossible for foreigners to solve or even to make a visible dent in India's higher education system.

Foreign institutions, once they realize the challenges of the Indian environment are unlikely to jump in a big way. Some may wish to test the waters. Many others will be deterred by the conditions put into place by Indian authorities and the uncertainties of the local situation.

The involvement of foreign higher education providers in India is perhaps just as murky as it was prior to Minister Sibal's new regime.

[*IHE* 60, Summer 2010]

About the Author and Coauthors

AUTHOR

Philip G. Altbach is J. Donald Monan, S.J. University Professor and director of the Center for International Higher Education in the Lynch School of Education at Boston College. He was the 2004–2006 Distinguished Scholar Leader for the New Century Scholars initiative of the Fulbright program and in 2010 was an Erudite Scholar of the Government of Kerala in India. His most recent book, coedited with Jamil Salmi, is *The Road to Academic Excellence: The Making of World-Class Research Universities*. He is author of *Turmoil and Transition: The International Imperative in Higher Education, Comparative Higher Education, Student Politics in America*, and other books. He coedited the *International Handbook of Higher Education*. Other recent books are *World Class Worldwide: Transforming Research Universities in Asia and Latin America, Leadership for World-Class Universities: Challenges for Developing Countries*, and *Trends in Global Higher Education: Tracking an Academic Revolution*.

COAUTHORS

Pawan Agarwal is education advisor at the Planning Commission, Government of India, New Delhi, India.

N. Jayaram is senior fellow at the Indian Institute of Advanced Study. Shimla, India. He has been dean of social sciences at the Tata Institute of Social Sciences, Mumbai.

Wanhua Ma is professor of education and director of the Center for International Higher Education, Peking University, Beijing, China.

Eldho Mathews is on the staff of the Planning Commission, Government of India, New Delhi, India.

Christine Musselin is director of the Centre de Sociologie des Organisations of the CNRS, and professor at SciencePo, Paris, France.

Iván F. Pacheco has been a research assistant at the Center for International Higher Education, Boston College.

Gerard A. Postiglione is head, Division of Policy, Administration, and Social Sciences, and director of the Wah Ching Center of Research on Education in China, University of Hong Kong.

Brendan Rapple is librarian at the O'Neill Library, Boston College.

Liz Reisberg is president of Reisberg & Associates, a consulting firm. She has been on the staff of the Center for International Higher Education at Boston College.

Jamil Salmi is a global tertiary education expert. He has been the World Bank's tertiary education coordinator.

Anthony Welch is professor of education at the University of Sydney, Sydney, Australia.

GLOBAL PERSPECTIVES ON HIGHER EDUCATION

Volume 1
WOMEN'S UNIVERSITIES AND COLLEGES
An International Handbook
Francesca B. Purcell, Robin Matross Helms, and Laura Rumbley (Eds.)
ISBN 978-90-77874-58-5 hardback
ISBN 978-90-77874-02-8 paperback

Volume 2
PRIVATE HIGHER EDUCATION
A Global Revolution
Philip G. Altbach and D. C. Levy (Eds.)
ISBN 978-90-77874-59-2 hardback
ISBN 978-90-77874-08-0 paperback

Volume 3
FINANCING HIGHER EDUCATION
Cost-Sharing in International perspective
D. Bruce Johnstone
ISBN 978-90-8790-016-8 hardback
ISBN 978-90-8790-015-1 paperback

Volume 4
UNIVERSITY COLLABORATION FOR INNOVATION
Lessons from the Cambridge-MIT Institute
David Good, Suzanne Greenwald, Roy Cox, and Megan Goldman (Eds.)
ISBN 978-90-8790-040-3 hardback
ISBN 978-90-8790-039-7 paperback

Volume 5
HIGHER EDUCATION
A Worldwide Inventory of Centers and Programs
Philip G. Altbach, Leslie A. Bozeman, Natia Janashia, and Laura E. Rumbley
ISBN 978-90-8790-052-6 hardback
ISBN 978-90-8790-049-6 paperback

Volume 6
FUTURE OF THE AMERICAN PUBLIC RESEARCH UNIVERSITY
R. L. Geiger, C. L. Colbeck, R. L. Williams, and C. K. Anderson (Eds.)
ISBN 978-90-8790-048-9 hardback
ISBN 978-90-8790-047-2 paperback

Volume 7
TRADITION AND TRANSITION
The International Imperative in Higher Education
Philip G. Altbach
ISBN 978-90-8790-054-4 hardback
ISBN 978-90-8790-053-3 paperback

Volume 8
THE PROFESSORIATE IN THE AGE OF GLOBALIZATION
Nelly P. Stromquist
ISBN 978-90-8790-084-7 hardback
ISBN 978-90-8790-083-0 paperback

Volume 9
HIGHER EDUCATION SYSTEMS
Conceptual Frameworks, Comparative Perspectives, Empirical Findings
Ulrich Teichler
ISBN 978-90-8790-138-7 hardback
ISBN 978-90-8790-137-0 paperback

Volume 10
HIGHER EDUCATION IN THE NEW CENTURY: GLOBAL
CHALLENGES AND INNOVATIVE IDEAS
Philip G. Altbach and Patti McGill Peterson (Eds.)
ISBN 978-90-8790-199-8 hardback
ISBN 978-90-8790-198-1 paperback

Volume 11
THE DYNAMICS OF INTERNATIONAL STUDENT CIRCULATION IN
A GLOBAL CONTEXT
Hans de Wit, Pawan Agarwal, Mohsen Elmahdy Said, Molatlhegi T. Sehoole,
and Muhammad Sirozi (Eds.)
ISBN 978-90-8790-259-9 hardback
ISBN 978-90-8790-258-2 paperback

Volume 12
UNIVERSITIES AS CENTRES OF RESEARCH AND KNOWLEDGE
CREATION: AN ENDANGERED SPECIES?
Hebe Vessuri and Ulrich Teichler (Eds.)
ISBN 978-90-8790-479-1 hardback
ISBN 978-90-8790-478-4 paperback

Volume 13
HIGHER EDUCATION IN TURMOIL: THE CHANGING WORLD OF
INTERNATIONALIZATION
Jane Knight
ISBN 978-90-8790-521-7 hardback
ISBN 978-90-8790-520-0 paperback

Volume 14
UNIVERSITY AND DEVELOPMENT IN LATIN AMERICA:
SUCCESSFUL EXPERIENCES OF RESEARCH CENTERS
Simon Schwartzman (Ed.)
ISBN 978-90-8790-524-8 hardback
ISBN 978-90-8790-523-1 paperback

Volume 22
TRENDS IN GLOBAL HIGHER EDUCATION: TRACKING AN
ACADEMIC REVOLUTION
Philip G. Altbach, Liz Reisberg and Laura E. Rumbley
ISBN 978-94-6091-338-9 hardback
ISBN 978-94-6091-339-6 paperback

Volume 23
PATHS TO A WORLD-CLASS UNIVERSITY: LESSONS FROM
PRACTICES AND EXPERIENCES
Nian Cai Liu, Qi Wang and Ying Cheng
ISBN 978-94-6091-354-9 hardback
ISBN 978-94-6091-353-2 paperback

Volume 24
TERTIARY EDUCATION AT A GLANCE: CHINA
Kai Yu, Andrea Lynn Stith, Li Liu, Huizhong Chen
ISBN 978-94-6091-744-8 hardback
ISBN 978-94-6091-745-5 paperback

Volume 25
BUILDING WORLD-CLASS UNIVERSITIES: DIFFERENT
APPROACHES TO A SHARED GOAL
Qi Wang, Ying Cheng, Nian Cai Liu
ISBN 978-94-6209-033-0 hardback
ISBN 978-94-6209-032-3 paperback

Volume 26
INTERNATIONALIZATION OF AFRICAN HIGHER EDUCATION –
TOWARDS ACHIEVING THE MDGs
Chika Sehoole, Jane Knight (Eds.)
ISBN 978-94-6209-310-2 hardback
ISBN 978-94-6209-309-6 paperback

Volume 27
THE INTERNATIONAL IMPERATIVE IN HIGHER EDUCATION
Philip G. Altbach
ISBN 978-94-6209-337-9 hardback
ISBN 978-94-6209-336-2 paperback

CPSIA information can be obtained at www.ICGtesting.com
Printed in the USA
BVOW06s0027230216

437703BV00002B/8/P